T0324457

THE NORTON SERIES ON
SOCIAL EMOTIONAL LEARNING SOLUTIONS
PATRICIA A. JENNINGS, SERIES EDITOR

*Mindfulness in the Secondary Classroom: A Guide for
Teaching Adolescents*
Patricia C. Broderick

*SEL Every Day: Integrating Social and Emotional Learning
with Instruction in Secondary Classrooms*
Meena Srinivasan

*Assessing Students' Social and Emotional Learning:
A Guide to Meaningful Measurement*
Clark McKown

*Mindfulness in the PreK–5 Classroom:
Helping Students Stress Less and Learn More*
Patricia A. Jennings

*Preventing Bullying in Schools:
A Social and Emotional Learning Approach to Early Intervention*
Catherine P. Bradshaw and Tracy Evian Waasdorp

NORTON BOOKS IN EDUCATION

Preventing Bullying in Schools

A Social and Emotional Approach to Early Intervention

**CATHERINE P. BRADSHAW and
TRACY EVIAN WAASDORP**

W. W. Norton & Company

Independent Publishers Since 1923

New York | London

Note to Readers: Models and/or techniques described in this volume are illustrative or are included for general informational purposes only; neither the publisher nor the author(s) can guarantee the efficacy or appropriateness of any particular recommendation in every circumstance.

CPB: To my daughter, Sophia Lucille McCaughey, for being a great inspiration to my work and life.

TEW: To my Mom and Dad for always pushing me higher. To Jon, Benji, and Alex for keeping me grounded.

Contents

From the Series Editor

The SOCIAL AND EMOTIONAL LEARNING SOLUTIONS (SEL SOLU-
TIONS) series features compact books for educators focused on recommended SEL practices from experts in the field. Cutting-edge research
continues to confirm that teaching students social and emotional skills pays
off in improved behavior and academic learning that continues into adulthood as success in life. The books are intended to provide school leaders
and classroom teachers with SEL tools and strategies that are grounded in
research yet highly accessible, so readers can confidently begin using them
to transform school culture, improve student behavior, and foster learning
with the proven benefits of SEL.

I am delighted to introduce this new book by Catherine Bradshaw and
Tracy Waasdorp entitled *Preventing Bullying in Schools: A Social and Emotional Learning Approach to Early Intervention* As a former teacher and school
leader, I recognized the value of allowing students to resolve their own con-

flicts. I understood that learning how to resolve peer conflict is an important part of school. However, it was often difficult to distinguish between normal peer conflicts and truly abusive behaviors. Furthermore, I wasn't sure how to successfully address these behaviors, and was afraid I might make things worse by interfering.

I recall watching one student act in an overbearing way towards a peer and asking myself, "Is this bullying? Should I intervene, and how?" I recognized the value of students learning to stand up for themselves and I was concerned that if I intervened in the wrong way, I would take the power away from the victim and possibly set her up for more abusive behavior in the future when I wasn't looking. If I didn't respond, the behavior might intensify, possibly reinforcing the victim and perpetrator roles. I knew that forcing the aggressor to apologize was not a productive strategy, but I wasn't sure what to do.

It can be challenging to sort through the research literature to find answers to such questions. In this book, Bradshaw and Waasdorp distill this research into effective and practical approaches you can use in your classroom to successfully prevent and address bullying behavior. Bullying is a complex problem that takes place in the context of schools, homes, media, and society. Social media presents a new venue for aggression that must be monitored by schools and families to ensure children's safety.

Preventing Bullying in Schools provides educators with the knowledge and research-based strategies to proactively approach bullying in their schools. The book explains the underlying causes of bullying and the serious long-term effects bullying can have on development for both the child who experiences bullying and the child who engages in such behavior. The book presents the most current research on how to help children who bully and those who experience bullying develop the social and emotional skills they need to successfully interact with their peers. These skills include understanding their emotions and how to communicate their needs to others, understanding others' perspectives, showing empathy, and resolving conflict successfully.

The book also provides important information about how to cultivate and maintain a supportive classroom climate that involves emotionally supportive relationships and interpersonal interactions that promote prosocial behavior. This valuable book delivers a sophisticated yet simple multicomponent approach to preventing bullying and skillfully intervening when it occurs. The book includes examples of successful strategies in the form of vignettes that are easy to quickly grasp and apply in your classroom. I am excited to present this useful book to the education community and am certain it will make a valuable contribution to improving the lives of children and their families by stemming the problematic behavior we call bullying.

Patricia A. Jennings, M.Ed., Ph.D.
Editor, Norton Series on Social and Emotional Learning Solutions

Acknowledgments

We would like to thank our colleagues, including Elise Pas, Steve Leff, Katrina Debnam, and many others on our research teams at the Johns Hopkins School of Public Health, the University of Virginia, and the Children's Hospital of Philadelphia who have supported and been a part of our research related to bullying and its prevention over the past 15 years. We would also like to thank Stephanie Tuman, Becca Seltzer, Christine Waanders, Brandy DeRosa, and Emily Solari for providing us with input that informed some of the vignettes included in the book.

Preventing Bullying in Schools

Bullying:
It Isn't Just Child's Play

Jane, an elementary school teacher who has been working for four years, tells her class to break into groups of four to five students to work on a STEM project at their tables. The assignment she was giving her class had them sharing materials and working on an experiment together. Jane told her students to select partners to work with who are sitting near them. After giving them a minute to get organized, she walks around to see if they have figured out their groups. Jane overhears one girl telling a boy (who was overweight and beginning to have body odor/hygiene issues) that he can't join their group. The girl says, "Ew, Thomas—you can't work with us. Go over there." The other students in the class laugh quietly to each other, and hold their noses or roll their eyes. Jane notices that Thomas is upset—he is clearly fighting back tears as he walks

1

away and approaches a different group. Jane has noticed this type of interaction is becoming a pattern, with the kids in her class saying mean things about Thomas with increasing frequency. She is struggling with how to help him fit in better.

As educators, we spend most of our time with kids, and we see a lot of concerning peer behaviors firsthand. Sadly, bullying and other forms of aggressive behavior are a major distraction in our schools. In fact, nearly one-third of students in the United States report being involved with bullying on a regular basis. And by the time they graduate high school, nearly all students have had personal experience with bullying—as either a bully, a victim, or a witness to it.

Because of its prevalence, bullying is something we hear a lot about; it's a term people throw around lightly. But what is it, exactly? We'll explore the nuances of bullying behaviors more fully in Chapter 2, but here we briefly set some parameters:

- Bullying typically occurs between two or more individuals in the context of a power or status differential.
- It is intentional and tends to happen over and over again.
- It can happen in person or online.
- It can take many forms, including leaving someone out on purpose,

spreading rumors, name calling, threatening physical or emotional harm, even stealing personal belongings.

It isn't just child's play. In fact, a number of studies have documented how bullying can have serious consequences. In addition to the more immediate impacts that are wreaking havoc on our schools, classrooms, youth clubs, sports teams, and online environments, it can also impact the way kids respond to stress, their memory, and their sleep patterns, not to mention their mental health and likelihood of engaging in risky behaviors (Copeland et al., 2014; National Academies of Sciences, 2016; Vaillancourt, Sanderson, Arnold, & McDougall, 2017).

Given all of this, it is not surprising that bullying can also cause students to be distracted from academics, make them concerned about their safety, and leave them feeling disconnected from their classmates and the school more broadly. Many bullied students start to "check out" mentally from school. They also start to miss school or skip class regularly. Another impact of bullying that is often overlooked is how it affects those who may witness the bullying as bystanders. Students who witness bullying are often distressed by these behaviors and concerned about intervening for fear they will be targeted next, do the wrong thing, or get into trouble. As a result, most kids who witness bullying simply do nothing or ignore it, as that often seems easier or safer to them than intervening or trying to get help from an adult (Bistrong, Bottiani, & Bradshaw, 2019; Waasdorp & Bradshaw, 2018).

As educators, we are often on the front lines of these issues, seeing bullying in our classrooms, hallways, and playgrounds. Yet most of us feel ill-equipped to respond effectively. It is a difficult dilemma: how to handle these challenging behaviors in real time, without making things worse. There may be a desire to use disciplinary strategies that largely focus on punishing kids who bully others. Yet there is little evidence that reactive and punitive approaches like suspension actually break this cycle or do much to stem these behaviors in the long run. Another common strategy is to demand a forced apology from the student who is bullying; but it is unrealistic to expect bullies and their victims to just shake hands and make up, or to resolve the disagreement on their own (Bradshaw, 2015). Adults who take this approach may be sending a message that bullying is just a mistake or misunderstanding, but it is much more complex and hurtful than a simple disagreement.

What is effective, instead, is a proactive approach that focuses on helping children who bully and those who experience bullying develop more effective social and emotional skills for interacting with peers, understanding their emotions, communicating their needs to others, and developing alternative means for attaining their goals. Also important is a supportive climate that emphasizes connections between people—relationships involving not only students, but parents, teachers, and other adults—and an overall sense of connection to the school and classroom. Together, these factors highlight the importance of using a multicomponent approach to bullying prevention and intervention, which considers multiple aspects of the student, the classroom, school, family—even the broader social context that affects us all through the media, social media, and politics (Bradshaw, 2015).

About This Book

The issue of bullying prevention is well aligned with the focus of the Norton Series on Social and Emotional Learning Solutions, in which this book is included. A large and growing body of research highlights the role of social and emotional learning (SEL) in relation to bullying and its prevention (Divecha & Brackett, 2019). Social and emotional learning is also a broader approach for working with students across settings and content areas to foster people and social skills. In fact, SEL approaches are effective for helping students with a range of challenges they may navigate, like stress, disappointment, peer rejection, academic problems, peer conflict—even exposure to traumatic events. Examples of SEL approaches that are often used with children include: learning ways to control your own emotions (emotional self-control), how to express feelings and be aware of how others are feeling, how to show empathy and put "yourself in someone else's shoes" (perspective taking), and the development of problem solving skills (e.g., resolving conflict).

Several rigorous research studies have documented both long- and short-term impacts of social and emotional programming on a range of outcomes including academic performance, behavior problems, and social skills (Durlak, Weissberg, Dymnicki, Taylor, & Schellinger, 2011; Taylor,

Oberle, Durlak, & Weissberg, 2017). This research suggests that dedicating teachers' and students' time and effort to implementing SEL programs and strategies is a good return on investment. But it's time consuming to wade through the research in search of answers to pressing problems, and we know educators have little time to spare. In this book, we leverage the research on SEL to provide concrete solutions, strategies, and approaches that educators can use in real time to address bullying behaviors and the problems they cause.

While this book tackles the issue of bullying in school most directly, it is important to recognize that SEL can have far-reaching impacts for students well beyond the classroom and across a variety of concerns. For example, we often think of bullying as something that just affects children and school-aged kids; however, various forms of bullying show up throughout adulthood (Bradshaw, 2017). Take for example social media and even news coverage of politicians, athletes, or television stars; often these news stories highlight some type of an abuse of power to influence others to do something, or more simply to inflict harm on others. This can take the form of workplace bullying, dating violence, sexual harassment, or other forms of harassment. These actions share commonalities with bullying: they use aggressive means of exerting power over others and often occur over and over again. Not surprisingly, bullying has longer-term impacts as well, which can cause serious mental health and relationship problems well into adulthood. As such, bullying is a complex phenomenon that can significantly impact both kids and adults. Moreover, there is compelling evidence that the roots of these problematic patterns of behavior lie in childhood and adolescence. One of the nuanced aspects of bullying behaviors that we explore is its ripple effects for both victims and kids who bully over the life course.

We begin this book in Chapter 2, by digging more into the definition of bullying and how it is conceptualized by youth and adults. We explore different forms of bullying, and contexts in which it occurs, with careful consideration of SEL and developmental factors. Since kids can engage in different roles in the bullying dynamic, we consider this more carefully in Chapter 3. In addition, we review some of the research on bullying, including risk factors and short- and long-term consequences. We also explore how different types of data can inform your use of different strategies, the need for professional development on this issue, and coaching supports that address bullying. We review additional research on the effects of bullying not only on students, but also on teachers and schools in Chapter 3. Consistent with this series, we examine this issue with an SEL lens, and in Chapter 4 we apply research findings in making recommendations for practical, effective strategies that can be used tomorrow in classrooms and schools. We provide suggestions for how you can talk with parents about bullying, and at the building level, on how to navigate policy-related issues and evaluate and sustain school-wide efforts. We further consider in Chapter 5 how regular use of these strategies will help you be better prepared to prevent bullying and other challenging behaviors before they happen, and know how to respond when they occur.

Identifying Bullying and the Roles Participants Play

Ty is a bit of a loner in his class and doesn't have many friends at school. He plays an online game after school every day as a way of interacting with other kids, even though he doesn't always know them in real life. A kid at school asks for his screen name, saying he wants Ty to join him and some other kids in another online game that afternoon. Soon after Ty logs on, excited to play the game with other students from his class, he realizes that his online profile avatar for the game has been altered to look like a naked monkey. He has been ambushed by the kid who invited him and five other kids in his class who also logged into the online game. He feels embarrassed, and logs off soon after. The next day at school, all the students in his class are making monkey noises and telling monkey-related jokes. Not only are the other kids' jokes hurtful, but his online gaming world, which was once a fun way to connect with others, no longer feels safe.

Bullying is broadly defined as intentional aggressive behavior that typically occurs repeatedly over time (or has the potential to be repeated) in the context of a power differential. Researchers have spent decades trying to get consensus on this definition and to outline specific criteria for what constitutes bullying and differentiates it from other types of problematic peer behavior, such as fighting, threatening, or conflict (Gladden, Vivolo-Kantor, Hamburger, & Lumpkin, 2014; Olweus, 1993).

Unpacking the Core Features of Bullying: RIP

While a technical definition of bullying is important on several levels, it may be most helpful to carefully consider a few nuances of bullying in greater detail. Later in this chapter, we consider the myriad forms that bullying can take, including the cyberbullying experienced by Ty in the vignette that opens this chapter. First, we unpack the broader definition into three core features, which we refer to as RIP: *repeated, intentional,* and *power.*

R for Repeated

One thing that makes bullying so hurtful is that it typically happens over and over again, often when kids least expect it. Bullying often occurs in cycles when it is frequent, is triggered by a targeted issue or a specific situation, and then can be mimicked by other kids. These issues can also follow kids across settings—occurring online, in person, at school, on the bus, or in the community. As such, bullying can be a 24-7 issue, given kids' access to social media and technology.

Defining bullying as repetitive can be confusing, as teachers often ask us if they should wait until the behavior happens again to intervene to make sure it is really bullying. And our answer is no, for regardless of whether it meets the technical definition of bullying, it is still hurtful and should be stopped. The earlier we adults intervene in these situations the better, as the risk of waiting is not worth the benefit of an accurate assessment of whether it really constitutes bullying or some other problematic behavior. This behavior has a high likelihood of being repeated and is probably hurtful, and thus should be stopped.

In the case of cyberbullying, a harmful email could be forwarded to multiple kids, resulting in wide distribution of hurtful lies or personal information. Similarly, posting personal and potentially damaging information on a social networking site or public website for many people to see also serves as a form of repetition consistent with this definition. As in the online gaming example at the start of this chapter, a behavior may occur only once, but without intervention, may be more likely to occur again or a pattern may emerge over time. For example, a bully may steal a student's lunch from her locker and eat it in front of others. Adults shouldn't wait until this happens again to intervene, as such behaviors can be very hurtful and lead to a variety of challenges if not addressed quickly and efficiently.

I for Intentional

Some students who bully will try to dismiss the behavior as an accident, a joke, or something they didn't mean to be harmful. While kids do make mistakes—bullying can take the form of a joke or start off as a game that goes too far—this is often a cover story for more intentional acts. The bully may simply be testing to see if the adult will dismiss it as an accident or conclude that it is just "kids being kids." It is important that adults not accept such an explanation uncritically and thus overlook potentially hurtful acts or dismiss them as accidents or just a game. Research suggests that kids who bully often take pleasure in putting others down and making them feel bad, as opposed to simply wanting to obtain a toy or other desired item. Rather, most bullying is social or relational in nature, which brings us to the third feature: *power.*

P for Power

The power aspect of bullying is often the most complex element for adults to tune into; in general, it's difficult for adults to understand social dynamics among children and adolescents. However, a core feature of bullying is that it occurs in situations where there is a real or perceived power or status difference between the students involved. Differences may be physical, based on age, gender, strength, or grade level. But more often they reflect social status within a group, which can be related to a host of other issues: popularity, social influence, physical attractiveness, weight, even socioeconomic status. Interestingly, online bullying, often referred to as cyberbullying, requires some skills in navigating the chosen technology— be it Twitter, Facebook, Snapchat, or other apps or programs. Not all kids know how to use these technologies, giving those who do greater power to leverage their skills to inflict harm. Thus the stereotypical computer geek is no longer inherently inferior to others when it comes to bullying. Other causes of low social power could be related to immigration status, having a disability (e.g., autism, learning disability, physical disability), belonging to an ethnic or racial minority, being gender nonconforming or identifying as LGBTQ. The list of possible differences that can make kids a target is extensive. Students who are at elevated risk of being victimized by their peers may be included in legally protected groups; thus it is important to carefully consider whether a bullying behavior may constitute harassment (Cornell & Limber, 2015). Regardless of whether the victims of bullying belong to protected classes or groups of students, educators must distinguish bullying from other problematic behaviors, like fights, disagreements, or conflict. As we've noted, not all negative acts constitute bullying; peer conflict, for instance, can simply be a disagreement or an argument that does not rise to the level of bullying. Individuals who are bullied have difficulty defending themselves due to the power or status difference that is a hallmark of bullying, making timely adult intervention critical.

How Common Is Bullying?

Peer bullying is the most common form of aggression that school-aged kids experience. It is estimated that about one-third of U.S. students are involved in bullying. For example, a survey of students in grades 9–12 by the U.S. Department of Education and the Department of Justice found that approximately 21% of students reported being bullied (in the past school year; Zhang, Musu-Gillette, & Oudekerk, 2016). A national survey of 4,000 U.S. children examined different bullying behaviors, finding that 48.2% of kids aged 10–13 (approximately middle school–age) experienced relational forms of aggression (e.g., spreading rumors or using exclusion to harm), and 8.6% encountered physical intimidation during the year (Finkelhor, Turner, Shattuck, & Hamby, 2015). Notably, while the topic of the study was bullying, the authors indicated they did not limit their results to instances involving a pattern of repetition or a power imbalance. Thus their definition of bullying differed from ours. A more recent study of over 240,000 students from 109 Maryland schools that examined self-reported bullying trends across 10 years found that between 13.4% and 28.8% of students in grades 4–12 reported that they experienced bullying (two or more times within the past month; Waasdorp, Pas, Zablotsky, & Bradshaw, 2017).

Researchers have found that when kids are asked about bullying in general, they tend to underreport it. However, rates of reported bullying rise when students are asked if they experienced specific behaviors; for example, where students can check Yes or No from a list of behaviors such as '*ignored or left out on purpose*' or '*hit, kicked, pushed*' in answer to the question "In what way were you bullied during the past 30 days?" (for additional examples see Sawyer, Bradshaw, & O'Brennan, 2008). In another study of almost 6,000 middle schoolers, between 34.5% and 44.1% kids responded to a more general question about whether they had been bullied, but that rate jumped up to nearly 50% when they were asked about specific bullying behaviors, like being teased, hit, or left out on purpose (Huang & Cornell, 2016). Taken together, these findings suggest that approximately 30% to 40% of students report moderate or frequent victimization via traditional (i.e., in-person) bullying. Moreover, experiencing two or more bullying incidents within a month is a common threshold for bullying to be considered frequent, which is typically associated with more harmful effects compared to less frequent bullying (see, for example, Bradshaw, Sawyer, & O'Brennan, 2007; Solberg & Olweus, 2003).

The Roles Students Play

Nessa was popular, pretty, and often the leader both in the classroom and in more social settings, like on the playground and during lunch. When the teacher assigned group work or allowed students to select where they sat in class, many of the other kids in the class would often want to work with or be in a group with her, especially the other girls in the class. One day, the teacher overheard what

Nessa was saying to the other kids during a group work assignment, and realized that she was talking meanly about kids in other groups. For example, she would comment about another student's clothes or the way they talked. The teacher started to pay more attention to Nessa and noticed a pattern. The teacher thought the students were all friends, but she soon realized that Nessa was essentially deciding who would be in her group each day. Although the groups would rotate, it appeared that one or two girls who weren't selected to be in the group would be picked on or left out of other social activities and interactions for the whole day. The teacher was surprised to learn that the group of kids selected each time would change from day to day, but they always followed Nessa's lead and laughed at or mimicked her teasing/exclusion behaviors. Although it was clear other students disliked what Nessa did and said about others, they did not try to stop her—likely because they were afraid of her and worried that they might be targeted next. The "followers" would do this even if they were on the receiving end the week before.

As can be seen in the situation with Nessa, students take on different roles when bullying occurs: the leader who instigated the bullying behavior, those who are victims, those who both perpetrate and are victims, and those who witness the behavior. It is not always easy to identify what roles students play in a bullying dynamic, and in fact, even kids who are popular can be the bullying ringleader. Below we will explain in more detail about these various involvement roles.

Bullies, Victims, and Bully-Victims

Although some students are largely instigators of bullying, whereby they bully others either independently or as part of a group, a greater number of students are victims of bullying. Although the vast majority of kids have experienced some form of bullying by the time they graduate from high school, only a fraction are frequent victims. This group of victims includes two common types, passive or reactive. Passive victims tend to react to bullying with internalized responses, like anxiety (Carrera, DePalma, & Lameiras, 2011), whereas reactive victims respond to their victimization with aggression. Less commonly, a child may play the role of both bully and victim. These kids, who are victims of bullying but also bully others, are typically referred to as bully-victims. They tend to experience the most adjustment problems, often as a consequence of their involvement in bullying (e.g., Holt et al., 2015; Valdebenito, Ttofi, Eisner, & Gaffney, 2017). We consider these issues in greater detail in Chapter 3, where we review some of the consequences of bullying using an SEL framework.

Bystanders

Although the central players in a bullying situation are typically the victim(s) and the perpetrator(s), bullying rarely occurs without the involvement of other peers as witnesses or bystanders (Hymel, McClure, Miller, Shumka, & Trach, 2015; Salmivalli, 2010). As can be seen in the story at the start of this section, the students selected by Nessa to be in the group were necessary in order for her to maintain the bullying; she needed people to follow her lead. This was also the case with the boy who was ambushed while playing an online game. These bystanders, although not the instigators, are clearly a driving force for the likelihood of the behavior continuing and for increasing the emotional impact the bullying will have on the victim. It is estimated that a bystander is present in nearly 90% of bullying instances (Craig, Pepler, & Atlas, 2000; Craig & Pepler, 1998). Sadly, most of these bystanders just passively observe the bullying without intervening or getting help (Bistrong et al., 2019; Waasdorp & Bradshaw, 2018).

By definition, bystanders are not directly involved as bullies or as victims, yet their behaviors can strongly impede or facilitate bullying (e.g., Kärnä, Voeten, Poskiparta, & Salmivalli, 2010). For instance, when a fight breaks out on the other side of the playground, some kids just ignore it, whereas others may run over to watch and cheer on the bully, and still others might try to break up the fight. This helps to illustrate the three main types of bystanders (Pöyhönen, Juvonen, & Salmivalli, 2012; Waasdorp & Bradshaw, 2018):

- *Contributors* act as an audience or follow the bully. Behaviors include laughing at something a bully did to a victim, liking a harmful social media post, following the bully's orders to exclude a victim, or huddling with a group of peers to surround and watch a bully and a victim.
- *Defenders* support the victim. Behaviors include trying to stop the

bullying, comforting the victim, reporting a harmful post, and getting an adult.

- *Passive bystanders* try to stay out of the bullying. Behaviors include seeing the bullying but walking away or doing nothing, trying to stay out of it, and ignoring the bullying.

There is considerable interest in trying to encourage bystanders to make more active and prosocial "upstander" responses to bullying (i.e., defender behavior). As witnesses, they have particular perspectives and potential influence over their peers that may make them an important leverage point for intervention.

Forms of Bullying

A fourth grade teacher had caught two students, Jeff and Brian, cheating in his classroom. The teacher knew that Brian was popular while Jeff was frequently picked on. The teacher pulled the students in separately. Jeff told the teacher that Brian said he would stop teasing Jeff if he let him cheat off of him, and added that if Jeff didn't comply with the cheating, Brian would make his life even more miserable than it was already and "really make him hurt."

Camille went to her second grade teacher during lunch crying about a situation involving one of her classmates, Isabella. Isabella was talking about her upcoming birthday which would be at a new venue in town—a play center with trampolines and obstacle courses. Isabella said to the other girls at the table, "Guess what? You are all invited to my party!" She deliberately skipped over Camille when handing out the invitations during lunch, saying, "Everyone except you—you are not invited."

Bullying often takes one of three forms: physical, verbal, or relational. *Physical* bullying involves behaviors such as hitting, pushing, and shoving. This behavior is overt, with a clear beginning and end. *Verbal* and *relational* bullying are both nonphysical forms of bullying. Verbal bullying involves overt behaviors such as face-to-face name-calling, teasing, and insults. In the first story above, Jeff was verbally bullied and constantly picked on and threatened. The second story about Camille involves relational bullying, which includes behaviors that damage relationships or social status such as rumors, gossip, withdrawal of friendship, and social exclusion (Crick & Grotpeter, 1995). While relational bullying can be direct (e.g., overtly telling someone they are not invited to a party, as in this case, or indirect (e.g., spreading rumors), direct relational bullying is more likely to occur between younger children. Relational bullying gets progressively more covert across the school years (Coyne & Ostrov, 2018).

Cyberbullying

Over 95% of U.S. teens (ages 13–17) have access to smartphones; 11% of these kids report they don't use these types of technologically-mediated interactions often (i.e., about once a day to several times a week). However, 44% of teens report using smartphones several times a day, and another 45% report using them almost constantly (Anderson & Jiang, 2018).

The increasing use of technology to interact with peers means that bullying may also occur through various digital electronic means. Cyberbullying, as it is often called, is defined by the medium through which verbal or relational bullying occurs (Gladden et al., 2014). However, whether cyberbullying is a distinct form is debated in the literature. Some claim that perpetrators and victims of cyberbullying are a unique subgroup, while others suggest this is not the case (Olweus, 2012; Patchin & Hinduja, 2012). Students who experience face-to-face bullying are also most likely to be victims of cyberbullying. Although cyberbullying may seem to impact a considerable number of victims, a large study of high school–age kids found that the majority of victims of bullying (75%) did not report experiencing cyberbullying; and only 4.6% experiencing *only* cyberbullying (Waasdorp & Bradshaw, 2015). It is rare that a victim of cyberbullying has never experienced any form of traditional in-person bullying. The consensus in the literature is that kids who experience cyberbullying also tend to experience it in person, highlighting a significant overlap in these forms of victimization.

Yet it is clear that cyberbullying is a distinctive experience for both the child who bullies and the victim. Although the same three broad defining criteria for in-person bullying apply to cyberbullying as well, there are some caveats. As we've seen, a power differential is at work in all forms of bullying: perpetrators have more physical power or higher social status than their victims. Cyberbullying has a twist: merely remaining anonymous (e.g., creating a fake online persona) or having advanced technological skills can create a power imbalance that might not pertain to face-to-face interactions between the bully and victim (e.g., Law, Shapka, Hymel, Olson, & Waterhouse, 2012; Waasdorp, Horowitz-Johnson, & Leff, 2017). Also, cyberbullying may not necessarily have to occur two or more times a month to be repetitive. For example, one humiliating picture posted online can be viewed by numerous individuals across a number of days. Thus, a single harmful cyberbullying behavior can revictimize without repeated incidents in a way that is peculiar to the online environment. We don't yet know if there is a threshold for cyberbullying where discernible harmful effects begin. It could be that one extreme incident is enough to cause harm, or it could be that a certain number of disparaging texts, posts, etc. need to be experienced in order to cause harm. It is also unknown as to what specific electronic content is "harmful enough" that they become noticeable to peers, parents, or other adults such as teachers. Therefore it is important to attend to and quickly intervene in any and all instances of cyberbullying, regardless of whether it occurs at school, at home, or in the community (Waasdorp, Mehari, & Bradshaw, 2017; Williford et al., 2013).

Bullying Across Stages of Development

Bullying behaviors can occur at any point across the life course, from early childhood through adulthood (Bradshaw, 2017). In fact, bullying-type behaviors have been found in children as young as 3. However, behaviors that include all the defining elements of bullying—characterized by repetition, power differential, and intent to harm—are not typical of young children's understanding and displays of aggression (Monks & Smith, 2006; Vaillancourt, McDougall, et al., 2008).

Bullying in Early Childhood

During free-play time at a preschool, a group of three girls usually chose to play house. One girl, India, tended to dominate the play. She was an influential and popular kid in the class. Each day, different kids would approach the playhouse to join in the play. Not only did India tell the other kids what their roles would be: "Ian, you be the dad. I'm going to be the mom. You can be the sisters . . ." she often picked one child who had to pretend to be in trouble and sit in the corner. Some kids would do what she told them and just sit there or receive their "punishment"; others would try to suggest other ideas, at which point she would say, "No, that's dumb. You need to do this." This often led to tears and frustration for kids in the class.

As we've noted, the intent to harm is key to defining bullying behavior; however, it's difficult to ascertain the true intent behind the aggressive behavior of young children, since their cognitive abilities are not fully developed. They may lack social-emotional skills to regulate their emotions or verbal skills to communicate their goals and feelings, and therefore resort to physical means to obtain things or status within a group. While it is common for preschool-aged children to use aggression to get their own needs met, such as getting a toy or a spot in line (Bistrong, Bradshaw, & Morin, 2016), repeated aggressive behavior among young children can be viewed as a precursor to bullying (Levine & Tamburrino, 2014). This repeated aggressive behavior is often spread across a variety of victims, as opposed to one specific victim (Saracho, 2017). For example, a group of preschoolers may regularly leave out a student in group role plays or games, saying hurtful things like "you can't play with us," "there isn't room for you to play with us," or "you should play with someone else instead." While these statements may seem relatively harmless, if they happen over and over again, they can be very hurtful and lead to a pattern of rejection and social aggression.

In fact, during the preschool years, precursory bullying behaviors often include these types of direct verbal and relational aggression, illustrated in the scenario with India at the start of this section. Such behaviors in preschool are associated with increased aggression throughout childhood (e.g., Ialongo, Vaden-Kiernan, & Kellam, 1998), underscoring the importance of early intervention. Regardless of whether we label these problem behaviors bullying, an early onset of these concerns (as either a bully or a victim) is a significant risk factor for subsequent adjustment problems.

Drawing on the large body of literature on the negative outcomes associated with an early onset of aggressive behavior, we urge educators to be sensitive to these issues and to seek assistance for children showing an early tendency toward bullying behavior, as it may suggest a trajectory of problem behaviors to come (Arseneault et al., 2006; Moffitt, 2006).

Middle Childhood Through Adolescence

In general, bullying rates are highest during the middle school years (approximately 10–13 years old) and tend to decrease by high school (Bradshaw et al., 2007; Hymel & Swearer, 2015; Waasdorp, Pas, et al., 2017). There is an exception to this trend, however: cyberbullying experiences may remain frequent across the high school years, largely because students have greater access to technology—much of which is unsupervised by adults (Waasdorp & Bradshaw, 2015).

As children mature cognitively, socially, and emotionally, physical bullying behaviors decrease, while verbal and relational bullying increases. Current research suggests that over time, children who bully tend to target a restricted number of victims: specifically, victims who are emotionally reactive (Haltigan & Vaillancourt, 2014).

Risk Factors for Bullying

Liam, a third grader, had just moved to North Carolina a week before school started because of his mom's new job. Having always lived in California and grown up with the same group of kids, they didn't focus on Liam only having four fingers on his left hand—which was the result of a birth defect. But in his new classroom, Liam became the target of bullying by nearly all the other students in the class. One day, a female student in the class wrote the following on a sticky note and put it on his Friday folder: "I am so sorry that Matt was laughing at you today because of your four fingers."

Childhood and adolescence is a time when feeling connected, accepted, and similar to peers is central; this normal drive to develop a self-identity can put kids at risk for victimization. One of the most commonly cited reasons for being bullied by peers is being perceived as different. Merely being shorter than average, wearing glasses, or even having asthma can increase a child's risk of being bullied. Certain individual characteristics, such as emotional or physical disabilities and gender-related factors, have been consistently found to increase the risk of victimization (e.g., Blake, Lund, Zhou, Kwok, & Benz, 2012; Pinquart, 2017; Waasdorp, Mehari, & Bradshaw, 2018). In this section we consider a few such factors that educators should keep in mind as they work to detect bullying in the classroom and protect potential targets.

Gender and Sexuality

> Chelsea is a sixth grader currently questioning her sexual orientation and gender identity. She has always been the target of bullying, for as long as she could remember—most likely because she wasn't like other girls. She didn't wear pink or play with dolls; instead she preferred playing soccer and basketball. She grew up in a home with all brothers. She was the youngest of five, and just preferred being with boys more than girls. She often wore her brothers' hand-me-downs and kept her hair short. The other kids often teased her and called her gay. Chelsea soon began to withdrawal from things she enjoyed, like sports, and started to skip school and avoid social events where other students from her class would be present. Her gender non-conforming behavior and appearance made her the target of bullying by her peers.

Bullying has been linked closely with gender. The research generally concludes that boys are more likely to bully others than are girls (Álvarez-García, García, & Núñez, 2015). Yet there may be some important gender differences in the form of bullying. In a national study of 12–18-year-old adolescents in the United States in 2013, more girls reported being bullied at school in the previous year compared to boys (24% vs. 19%; Zhang et al., 2016). Specifically, more girls reported being the victim of verbal behaviors like name-calling or insults, and more relational behaviors like rumors or intentional exclusion from activities. More boys reported being pushed, shoved, tripped, or spit on than girls (Zhang et al., 2016).

Historically, much of the bullying research has studied physical and verbal forms of bullying. Once relational forms of bullying were examined, additional kids were identified as perpetrators and victims, with a large proportion of those newly identified being girls (Putallaz et al., 2007). When girls bully, they are more likely to use relational as compared to physical forms; boys use both kinds of bullying (Coyne & Ostrov, 2018). Notably, the emotional distress and perception of harm related to the experience of relational bullying is higher for girls than for boys (Coyne, Archer, & Eslea, 2006; Crick, Bigbee, & Howes, 1996). For example, in a study of the association between the forms of victimization (including physical, verbal, and attacks on property, as well as social manipulation, which is a relational victimization behavior) and post-traumatic stress disorder (PTSD), social manipulation was most strongly associated with PTSD for girls; for boys, the overt form of attacks on property was most strongly associated with PTSD (Litman et al., 2015).

These findings are likely due in part to the gendered development of peer relationships (Maccoby, 1998; Martin, Fabes, Hanish, Leonard, & Dinella, 2011); boys and girls prefer same-sex friends during early childhood, a preference that continues throughout adolescence into adulthood (Mehta & Strough, 2009; Rose & Asher, 2017). Friendships have distinct features for girls and boys. Due to the partiality toward same-sex peers the differences in peer relationships, including bullying, are more pronounced across development (Maccoby, 1998; Martin et al., 2013). Boys often have larger peer groups that focus on games, whereas girls have smaller peer groups that are more intimate and focus on social conversations (Blatchford, Baines, & Pellegrini, 2003; Rose & Rudolph, 2006). Girls' peer relationships often have more self-disclosure and intimacy compared to those of boys. These reciprocal relationships are more important for girls (Hall, 2011; Hay & Ashman, 2003).

Children are more likely to use aggression with same-sex peers (Martin, Fabes, & Hanish, 2014; Pellegrini et al., 2007). When boys are the victims of bullying, the instigators are usually outside of their immediate peer group; however, for girls, the instigators are more often within their immediate peer group. In other words, a girl is more likely to be bullied by someone she considered a friend—and when aggression occurs among girls, they will have more intimate knowledge that can be used to harm other girls emotionally. Because girls place higher importance on peer relationships (Hay & Ashman, 2003; Ma & Huebner, 2008), becoming the target of relational bullying can be very detrimental (e.g., Vaillancourt, Duku, et al., 2008).

Finally, research is clear that children and teens who are gender nonconforming and/or belong to a sexual minority (such as lesbian, gay, bisexual, and transgender) are at an increased risk for being bullied (Goodenow, Watson, Adjei, Homma, & Saewyc, 2016; Toomey & Russell, 2016). In a national survey of over 5,000 kids between the ages of 13 and 18, sexual minority kids had extremely high odds of suicidal ideation (i.e., suicidal thoughts, or thinking or planning a suicide) (Ybarra, Mitchell, Kosciw, & Korchmaros, 2015), although these odds can be improved through feeling connected to an adult at school (Duong & Bradshaw, 2014). In states with general antibullying laws as well as specific laws that include sexual minorities as a protected class of people, these kids experience less bullying victimization (Seelman & Walker, 2018), further suggesting the important role of schools in reducing both the occurrence and the impact of bullying for at-risk kids.

Race and Ethnicity

The literature that compares bullying across race and ethnicity is somewhat mixed. Regarding those who bully, some research has found that it is more prevalent among African American students (Albdour & Krouse, 2014; Wang, Iannotti, & Nansel, 2009, but other research does not support this finding). While additional research is needed to better understand the association between race/ethnicity and bullying, it is clear that African American kids are more likely to be reported as aggressive by both peers and teachers compared to any other racial or ethnic group (Noguera, 2003). However, given that peers and teachers are often the source of information on bullying, the true differences between the experiences of bullying perpetration across these subgroups is currently unknown. It is therefore important to examine one's own biases that might influence perceptions of behavior in the classroom.

Regarding bullying victimization, the research is also mixed, with some studies showing no differences by race or ethnicity (e.g., Connell et al., 2015; Estell, Farmer, & Cairns, 2007). Others do show differences, such as a nationwide study in which a higher percentage of white adolescents reported being bullied compared to black, Hispanic, and Asian adolescents (Zhang et al., 2016). The incongruity in these results may be due to the way in which the research question was posed. Researchers use either behavioral (e.g., listing behaviors that constitute bullying but do not include the term bullying) or definitional methods (e.g., providing a definition of bullying) to assess bullying victimization. Behavioral methods revealed higher rates of victimization among African American teens and Asian boys than definitional methods (Sawyer et al., 2008). It is therefore important to keep in mind how bullying involvement data are collected at your school, as this can have an effect on whether certain populations of children are more or less likely to be identified as a bully or a victim. Notably, very few studies have specifically examined Asian and Latino/a teens, yet these populations likely have different risks and protective factors for involvement in bullying (Hong et al., 2014) such as being an immigrant and/or having parents who are not from the United States. Specifically, a study found that, compared to native-born kids, immigrant kids are significantly more likely to experience all forms of bullying (Maynard, Vaughn, Salas-Wright, & Vaughn, 2016). It is important to be aware that this population of kids might be at an increased risk for victimization.

Health-Related Factors

Subgroups of kids may be particularly vulnerable to bullying and victimization due to health-related conditions and behaviors. Students with visible differences related to a disability or condition are more likely to be bullied, for instance, than those who don't have such observable differences (Bradshaw et al., 2007; Pinquart, 2017; Swearer, Wang, Maag, Siebecker, & Frerichs, 2012).

Children and adolescents with chronic physical illnesses or disabilities (e.g., obesity, asthma, chronic skin diseases, visual impairment) are more likely to be victims of bullying: around 35%, compared to 26% of those without. Verbal bullying, such as teasing related to the disability or illness, is the most commonly reported bullying experience (Pinquart, 2017). Having a medical condition that interferes with day-to-day functioning may disrupt students' abilities to attend school regularly and to engage in activities, especially physical activities, with their peers (Faith et al., 2015). This decreased social integration may in turn create barriers to friendship formation, decrease social support, and increase stigma related to medical conditions (e.g., Alhaboby, Barnes, Evans, & Short, 2017; Faith et al., 2015).

Adolescents with asthma are more likely to be victimized both in person and online (Gibson-Young, Martinasek, Clutter, & Forrest, 2014; Waasdorp, Mehari, Milam, et al., 2018). A stigma related to having asthma (Wildhaber, Carroll, & Brand, 2012) could increase their risk of victimization. For example, kids may not be able to participate in sports teams or gym class, or even play outside. These restrictions could decrease their opportunities for positive peer interactions, as well as increase the likeli-hood that peers view the child as atypical. Asthma medications may cause side effects such as inattentiveness, difficulty concentrating, mood changes, poor time management (Naudé & Pretorius, 2003), and deficits in executive function, all of which can increase the risk of both victimization and bully-ing for students taking these medications (Faith et al., 2015).

Another group at an increased risk of victimization is kids who are obese or overweight (van Geel, Vedder, & Tanilon, 2014; Wildhaber et al., 2012). In fact, according to a large study, overweight middle and high school kids had almost 20% higher odds and obese kids had almost 60% higher odds of reporting being bullied in general compared to average-weight ado-lescents. Further, compared to average-weight kids, both overweight and obese kids were at an increased risk of relational, verbal, and cyber victim-ization, with only obese kids having an increased risk of physical victim-ization (Waasdorp, Mehari, & Bradshaw, 2018). Cultural stigma around weight may place obese and overweight kids at risk for being victimized (Cole-Lewis, Gipson, Opperman, Arango, & King, 2016; Puhl & Latner, 2007). Youth who are obese or overweight are less likely to be viewed as desirable friends and therefore have fewer friendships. Negative character traits, such as being lazy, stupid, and dirty, are more often attributed to these kids (Gray, Kahhan, & Janicke, 2009). In addition to increasing the risk of victimization by peers, being obese or overweight seems to also increase the likelihood that a student will engage in bullying themselves; being overweight has been associated with higher rates of bullying perpetration (Jansen et al., 2014; Pinquart, 2017; Waasdorp, Mehari, Milam, et al., 2018).

This is an important group of kids to watch when trying to prevent, detect, and address bullying behaviors.

The Role of Social and Emotional Factors in Bullying

Dylan is much less socially skilled than the other kids in the class. The teachers find him immature and often "clueless" about how to behave appropriately with peers. One day on the way to lunch, he hears another boy, DeShawn, say, "Dylan—those girls want you to sit with them today," while the kids standing near DeShawn all laugh at Dylan. He looks excited and goes toward the girls' table, only to be turned away. He looks upset, but keeps his head down and sits at a table by himself.

When engaging in various social interactions, particularly ones which are potentially stressful, conflictual, or ambiguous, children and adults alike go through a series of mental steps to create a response to the situation (Camodeca & Goossens, 2005; Crick & Dodge, 1994; Jenkins, Tennant, & Demaray, 2018). Specifically, there are five steps: (1 and 2) encoding and interpreting external and internal cues; (3) clarification of individual goals and desired outcomes; (4) thinking about what responses are possible; and (5) selecting a response (Crick & Dodge, 1994, 1996). In general, both perpetrators of aggression and victimized kids have difficulty with their perceptions of, or their reactions within, peer interactions (Cook, Williams, Guerra, Kim, & Sadek, 2010). Having poor social information processing skills places a child at risk for bullying and victimization as can be seen in the situation with Dylan and his classmates. Moreover, students who bully often think they have been the target of unfair behavior by others, and think their aggressive response is justified or appropriate given the context and history. In fact, youth who bully often complain that people are always "unfair to them"; they often think that they are just setting things straight, and thus justify or rationalize their own behavior in the context of fairness.

As we explore more closely in subsequent chapters, the social-emotional learning (SEL) framework helps us address many of the skills necessary to process social interactions successfully and develop and maintain positive social relationships. Therefore, we introduce this framework here to set the stage for conceptualizing SEL as a focal area for bullying prevention.

Consistent with work by the Collaborative for Academic, Social, and Emotional Learning (CASEL), we focus on the five broad SEL competencies: (1) self-awareness, (2) self-management, (3) social awareness, (4) relationship skills, and (5) responsible decision making, all of which play an important role in deciding how to respond to a bullying situation. These competencies are important skills necessary for academic and social success (e.g., Zins, Bloodworth, Weissberg, & Walberg, 2004; Zins, Payton, Weissberg, & O'Brien, 2007) and can also be a lens through which to examine the risk factors for involvement in bullying (Espelage, De La Rue, & Low, 2015; Smith & Low, 2013).

Self-awareness is defined as the ability to accurately recognize one's own emotions and thoughts, as well as their influence on behavior (Oberle & Schonert-Reichl, 2017; Yoder, 2014). The inability to identify or describe emotions (alexithymia) has been found to correlate with bullying. Specifically, in a sample of over 1,500 12–18-year-olds, children who reported in-person or cyberbullying behaviors had higher scores on an alexithymia scale than those who had never bullied. Those that reported both in-person bullying and cyberbullying had the highest scores (Wachs & Wright, 2018). Scholars argue that children who bully can cognitively process emotional information, but lack the ability to appreciate the emotional consequences of their behavior for others' feelings (e.g., Gini, 2006). Thus, it is important to increase these children's ability to be self-aware, through correctly recognizing their emotions, and, once recognized, to gain an understanding of how these emotions and their thoughts regarding the emotions can negatively impact their behavior.

Self-awareness also entails having an accurate self-perception, recognizing one's strengths, and feeling self-confident (see "Core SEL Competencies," n.d.; Yoder, 2014). Victims of bullying often have lower self-esteem and more negative self-concepts compared to nonvictimized peers (e.g., Boulton, Smith, & Cowie, 2010; Tsaousis, 2016). A meta-analysis found that the relationship between victimization and self-esteem is transactional: meaning that while peer victimization was clearly associated with lower self-esteem, having low self-esteem also increased the risk for victimization (van Geel, Goemans, Zwaanswijk, Gini, & Vedder, 2018). Some studies have also shown that children who bully have lower self-esteem and that lower self-esteem predicts bullying perpetration behaviors, whereas others suggest bullies have higher self-esteem and inflated self-perceptions, or that self-esteem is not related to bullying perpetration at all (Donnellan, Trzesniewski, Robins, Moffitt, & Caspi, 2005; Edalati, Afzali, & Conrod, 2018; Juvonen & Graham, 2014; Rose, Slaten, & Preast, 2017). This suggests that the association between perpetration and self-esteem is still unclear, challenging the often-believed notion that all children who bully have poor self-esteem. Nevertheless, an SEL focus on improving self-awareness would likely have a protective role for decreasing these risk factors for both victims and children who bully.

Self-management is defined as the ability to regulate emotions, thoughts, and behaviors (Yoder, 2014). An association between lack of emotion regulation, such as aggressive impulsivity and bullying behavior, has been found across elementary, middle, and high school (O'Brennan, Bradshaw, & Sawyer, 2009; van Geel, Toprak, Goemans, Zwaanswijk, & Vedder, 2017). While studies have shown that children who bully show problems with control such as impulsivity (e.g., Edalati et al., 2018; Verlinden et al., 2014), poor response inhibition is also associated with being a victim of bullying (Edalati et al., 2018; Jenkins et al., 2018). For example, children who have poorer regulation of sadness and anger along with general emotional instability are more likely to be victims (Cooley & Fite, 2016; Troop-Gordon, 2017). A highly emotional response to bullying that attracts a lot of attention likely increases the chance that the bullying will occur again.

Another aspect of self-management that is important for understanding bullying is the ability to manage stress ("Core SEL Competencies," n.d.; Yoder, 2014). The experience of being a victim can cause social and emotional stress, which can prove to be extremely taxing (Vaillancourt et al., 2017). Throughout development, children increasingly use peers to cope with stress, yet victims of bullying often have poorer social relationships and fewer positive friendships (e.g., Spriggs et al., 2007) and therefore, will likely not have the necessary social support (Troop-Gordon, 2017). Not only is a lack of supportive social relationships a risk factor, it is cyclical; children with fewer friends are more likely to be victims of bullying, and victims often have fewer friends (e.g., Wang et al., 2009). It is therefore important for victims of bullying to develop strategies for both making and maintaining friendships as well as develop stress management strategies that may not involve peers.

Social awareness is defined as the ability to empathize with and take the perspective of others. Empathy can fall into two categories: cognitive or affective empathy. Cognitive empathy includes perspective-taking skills and being able to understand another person's point of view, whereas affective empathy is the ability to feel how another person is feeling or vicariously sharing the emotion of another (Davis, 1983; Eisenberg & Miller, 1987). Studies show that some children who bully have stronger *callous-unemotional traits*, defined as an absence of empathy and guilt, constricted display of emotion, and the callous use of others for their own personal gain (e.g., Golmaryami et al., 2016; van Geel et al., 2017). Callous-unemotional traits are associated with lower levels of empathy (Frick, Ray, Thornton, & Kahn, 2014), and children who bully often have less empathy, both cognitive and especially affective empathy (Espelage, Hong, Kim, & Nan, 2018; van Noorden, Haselager, Cillessen, & Bukowski, 2015). The association is stronger for affective empathy, indicating that children who bully may have some ability to know or cognitively understand what the victim is feeling, but may not be adept at feeling what the victim is feeling (van Noorden et al., 2015).

Bully-victims express less general empathy for victims compared to children who bully but are not also victimized (e.g., Gini, Pozzoli, & Hauser, 2011; van Noorden, Cillessen, Haselager, Lansu, & Bukowski, 2017). A meta-analysis of empathy and bullying involvement found that children who are victims of bullying are lower on cognitive empathy but not affective empathy (van Noorden et al., 2015). This study also found that kids who are positive bystanders (i.e., use defender behaviors) have higher cognitive and affective empathy. The importance of differentiating and bolstering both cognitive and affective empathy skills is therefore key in reducing bullying behaviors.

Notably, compared to in-person bullying, cyberbullying shifts the notion of perspective taking in that the instigators and bystanders do not see the victim's response, increasing the ability for moral disengagement; that is, it allows children who bully to re-frame their behavior as morally acceptable given they do not *see* the emotional harm it is causing (Cross et al., 2015). Similar to in-person bullying, children who cyberbully have low affective and cognitive empathy (Zych, Baldry, Farrington, & Llorent, 2018). Cyberbullying also has the potential for more bystanders than in-person bullying (e.g., Schultze-Krumbholz & Scheithauer, 2013). Therefore, increasing both cognitive and especially affective empathy can be an effective method for reducing cyberbullying (Cross et al., 2015; Schultze-Krumbholz, Schultze, Zagorscak, Wölfer, & Scheithauer, 2016).

Relationship skills provide the ability to establish and maintain healthy relationships. Behaviors include the ability to communicate clearly, engage positively with others, and negotiate conflict constructively ("Core SEL Competencies," n.d.; Oberle & Schonert-Reichl, 2017). We know that both bullies and victims need assistance in enhancing relationship skills. All involved individuals—bystanders, children who bully, and victims—would benefit from increasing their communication skills, learning to negotiate conflict, and increasing problem-solving skills. Most programs for reducing bullying do focus on increasing problem-solving skills, conflict resolution, and assertive communication skills (e.g., Frey, Hirschstein, & Guzzo, 2000).

Responsible decision making, the final SEL skill, is the ability to make constructive choices about behavior and social interactions based on ethical standards, safety concerns, social and behavioral norms, and consequences ("Core SEL Competencies," n.d.; Oberle & Schonert-Reichl, 2017). This includes the ability to identify the problem and develop appropriate solutions (Yoder, 2014). Often both children who bully and their victims need assistance with this skill.

In summary, bullying is a significant concern affecting the majority of school-aged kids either directly or indirectly, with a myriad of risk factors for involvement in bullying. In this chapter, we focused on risk factors, largely at the individual level, that may increase the likelihood that students will engage in bullying—either as victims or perpetrators. We introduced the SEL model and five core competencies as a framework for conceptualizing the risk factors for bullying. This model informs the content of the next chapter, which considers the context of bullying and its impacts on children and the classroom. The SEL perspective also lays the foundation for subsequent chapters that focus more on strategies for intervening in bullying situations.

Understanding the Impact on Students, Teachers, and Schools

Mai, a fifth grade student who had just immigrated from Vietnam to the U.S., was pretty and smart. A group of popular girls almost immediately started calling her names, making fun of her non-fluent English, and targeting her looks and clothes. Mai did have a group of friends that welcomed her in the school, but as the school year progressed, the teasing got worse. The girls started spreading rumors about her, which ruined the friendships she did have. There was a boy in Mai's class who had been kind to Mai, but for fear he would become a target, was soon influenced by the girls who were bullying her to pretend to like her in order to get embarrassing texts and pictures, which they spread to all kids in the grade. The school staff noticed the teasing, but from their point of view there was no clear harm to Mai (no physical harm), so the behavior was regarded as "kids will be kids" and little adult intervention occurred. Teachers were also under a lot of pressure from administrators to raise test scores; the peer relationships of their students were not a top priority. When the teasing was distracting, one teacher pulled the group of them together (Mai and the 'ringleaders') and tried to get the kids to apologize to her. The kids apologized in front of the teacher but they did not shift their behaviors; in fact, the teacher's intervention made it worse. Many of the teachers would tell their students to 'leave the drama outside' in an effort to focus on academics, making Mai feel that while the teachers obviously saw what was happening (how could anyone miss it?) the teacher did not care about her situation at all. The kids who were bullying Mai knew they could get away with it; there were times where school staff would be witnesses to their taunting and merely tell Mai not to worry and repeat that old statement about 'sticks and stones can break my bones, but words can never hurt me.' Mai's parents saw her grades slipping and when they confronted her, Mai revealed she was being bullied. In conferences with teachers and administrators, Mai's parents expressed concern that they had not heard about anything that was going on, to which the school responded that they never received any discipline reports of Mai's situation. The administrators and school counselors assured her parents they would do everything they could to stop the bullying. The school counselor decided to put Mai in a small social skills group, where she interacted with other students who had a difficult time managing their emotions and making good choices, but also included some students with good social skills who served as role models. Although well-intended, these group sessions did little to stop the bullying, and Mai started to believe she was the problem. She felt completely alone.

Bullying does not occur in isolation; it is heavily influenced by its context. There are influences across multiple levels, from child-specific family influences, to peer and school staff influences, to broader social contextual influences (e.g., school-wide norms and societal norms; Espelage & Swearer, 2004; Gibson, Polad, Flaspohler, & Watts, 2016). Because all of these influences perpetuate or ameliorate bullying, it is not an individual problem, but a systemic problem. In Mai's situation, focusing on one instigator did not help alleviate the problem and neither did a social skills group solely focusing on her. Everyone around her seemed to be playing a role in perpetuating the bullying. Bullying has a ripple effect on all of those involved: the instigator and the victim, as well as bystanders, and more broadly on the classroom and school climate (e.g., Lindstrom Johnson, Waasdorp, Debnam, & Bradshaw, 2013; Waasdorp & Bradshaw, 2018). In this chapter, we consider the range of impacts of bullying from an SEL perspective.

The Impact on Individuals

Children Who Bully

Bullying perpetration is a significant predictor of later risky or illegal behavior, such as a two-thirds increased risk of violence (Ttofi, Farrington, & Lösel, 2012), and elevated risks for felonies and substance use (Wolke, Copeland, Angold, & Costello, 2013). In a sample of male students at age 14, those identified as perpetrators of bullying were at a higher risk for a violent conviction between the ages of 15 and 20, drug use at ages 27–32, and the perception of an unsuccessful life at age 48, as compared to those who were not involved (Farrington & Ttofi, 2011). In a longitudinal study extending to age 26, children who bullied had an increased likelihood of having violent relationships later in life as well as problems making or keeping friends (Wolke et al., 2013). Children who bullied had an increased risk for not attending or completing college, job dismissal, and quitting multiple jobs (Wolke et al., 2013).

Of course, not all children who bully have the same outcomes or similar patterns of behavior. For example, a study following students who bully from middle into high school found multiple subgroups of bullies. One group recorded the highest levels of bullying across middle school (grades 6, 7, and 8) and declining levels in high school; another group showed high levels in sixth grade only and a large decline in subsequent years; and finally another group started off low in sixth grade but progressively increased their bullying perpetration with each subsequent grade. This study also found that outcomes across perpetrators are not necessarily similar. The bullies in the latter two groups—who showed such different patterns across the middle and high school years—had the highest self-reported rates of delinquency (Espelage et al., 2018). It is helpful to keep in mind that we should not assume all children who bully do so for the same reasons or will follow a specific trajectory.

Victims of Bullying

The experience of being bullied is considered a serious traumatic event, evidenced by its association with PTSD (Litman et al., 2015), and through studies that isolate the causal link between being a victim in childhood and/or adolescence and negative outcomes over and above any prior risks that the child might have (e.g., Arseneault, 2018). Mai's story illustrates the pervasive experience of bullying and how it can lead a child to perceive she is somehow to blame. Studies of victims show that they are more likely to be depressed 36 years later as compared to noninvolved youth; being a victim of bullying is an even stronger predictor of depression than 20 other major childhood risks, including being friends with delinquent or aggressive peers, average family income/maternal education level, academic achievement, and childhood attention problems (Ttofi, Farrington, Lösel, & Loeber, 2011). A meta-analysis of 165 studies revealed that being a victim is strongly associated with mental health difficulties such as depression, anxiety, and suicidal ideation and attempts. For those who are bullied more frequently, the likelihood of these maladaptive outcomes is even stronger (Moore et al., 2017; Takizawa, Maughan, & Arseneault, 2014). A meta-analysis of 18 longitudinal studies revealed that peer victimization predicted later internalizing symptoms (negative, problematic behaviors directed toward the self); however, having internalizing symptoms also predicted peer victimization (Reijntjes, Kamphuis, Prinzie, & Telch, 2010). As the authors suggest, this indicates that internalizing symptoms can not only cause bullying victimization but can perpetuate continual victimization experiences.

The association between being the victim of bullying and poor mental health has even been found in twin studies where many environmental and genetic influences are similar (Arseneault et al., 2008; Silberg et al., 2016). Along with the emotional impacts of being a victim, there are negative social impacts well beyond school-age years. These include reports of economic hardship, few rewarding social relationships, and poor perceived quality of life at age 50 (Takizawa et al., 2014; Wolke et al., 2013). Studies have also found that victims of bullying are at an increased risk for substance use (e.g., alcohol, tobacco, illicit drugs; Moore et al., 2017) and violent behaviors (approximately six years later) compared to their uninvolved peers (Ttofi et al., 2012). Victims have an increased risk of health-related difficulties such as headaches, stomachaches, and difficulties sleeping (Moore et al., 2017; Waasdorp, Mehari, Milam, & Bradshaw, 2018). Victims are also at risk of poor academic outcomes (Moore et al., 2017). In a study that followed students ages 11–13 for two years, being the victim of bullying at the start of the study (when they were between the ages of 11–13) was associated with lower academic achievement in subsequent waves, and this early bullying victimization was linked with diminished academic achievement and was directly associated with higher levels of problem drinking and depression (Davis et al., 2018). Findings such as these suggest that victimization can cascade into other social, emotional, and behavioral difficulties.

Bully-Victims

Studies repeatedly find that those who are both victims and perpetrators of bullying, bully-victims, have the most maladaptive outcomes. For example, a study of over 24,000 elementary, middle, and high school students found that bully-victims were most likely to have internalizing symptoms, problems in peer relationships, and poorer perceptions of the school environment (O'Brennan, Bradshaw, & Sawyer, 2009). Longitudinal studies show that bully-victims have increased risks for later diagnosis of psychiatric disorders, drug use, and even poorer health outcomes such as serious illness and slow recovery from illness (Copeland, Wolke, Angold, & Costello, 2013; Wolke et al., 2013).

Although children who bully, victims of bullying, and bully-victims all have an increased risk of suicidal ideation and attempts, bully-victims had the highest risk of all three subgroups (Holt et al., 2015). Similarly, all three subgroups (bullies, victims, and bully-victims) had significantly increased risk of carrying a weapon to school, although bully-victims had the highest odds of the three subgroups (Valdebenito et al., 2017). Notably, although victims and bully-victims were likely to carry a weapon in school, only children who bully had higher odds of also carrying the weapon outside of school (Valdebenito et al., 2017). In Wolke et al.'s (2013) study, bully-victims had the highest risk of not receiving a college or high school diploma, quitting multiple jobs, and poverty. These students were also significantly more likely to have poor relationships with parents, lack a best friend, and have problems making or keeping friends. Bully-victims have lower academic achievement than both pure victims and pure bullies, with the highest likelihood of suspension or expulsion compared to bystanders (Glew, Fan, Katon, Rivara, & Kernic, 2005).

Bystanders

While being a positive bystander to bullying has been shown to help victims and stop bullying (Sainio, Veenstra, Huitsing, & Salmivalli, 2011; Salmivalli, Voeten, & Poskiparta, 2011), merely witnessing bullying can have an impact on the bystanders as well (e.g., Lambe, Hudson, Craig, & Pepler, 2017; Rivers, Poteat, Noret, & Ashurst, 2009). For example, in a study of over 5,000 fourth–12th graders, defending against bullying (through supporting the victim) was associated with social and emotional difficulties such as internalizing or psychosomatic symptoms (e.g., headaches, stomachaches); in schools with higher levels of bullying, these psychosocial difficulties increased (Lambe et al., 2017). The same study found that the negative effects of being a bystander were worse for boys who reported defending behavior compared to boys who reported witnessing the bullying only (and not defending).

While defending behaviors are desirable, not all defending behaviors are the same. Specifically, a three-year study of 394 fourth grade children examined both bully-oriented defending (e.g., chasing the bully away) and victim-oriented defending (e.g., consoling the victim). Three main patterns of defending behaviors emerged, with different effects on likeability and reputation. Children who were rated high on both defending behaviors were better liked and had higher social status, such that they were perceived as more popular and had more influence or control over resources. Children who defended using predominantly victim-oriented behaviors were well liked but had low reputations, whereas children who were predominantly bully-oriented in defending had higher reputations yet were disliked (Reijntjes et al., 2016). This suggests that while defending behaviors might help the victim, certain defending behaviors can place children at an increased risk for negative consequences. In a study of over 8,000 middle and high school students, both harmful and helpful bystander behavior was associated with internalizing symptoms. Being a harmful bystander (e.g., laughing at the victim, excluding someone that the bully wants excluded, huddling around to watch a physical bullying situation) was also associated with future aggressive behavior and decreased academic achievement, whereas positive bystander behavior was associated with higher academic achievement and higher self-esteem (Evans, Smokowski, Rose, Mercado, & Marshall, 2018). Taken together, while additional studies on psychological effects are necessary, current research suggests that witnessing bullying can be traumatic for bystanders, although for some youths, intervening through providing support for the victim can have a positive impact.

The Impact of Bullying on Classroom and School Climate

It is clear that bullying has an impact not only on the individuals involved but also on the broader social climate in a school (Cornell & Bradshaw, 2015). The bullying in Mai's school spread quickly; twice, Mai lost friends due to their fear they would be next. In a situation like this, the system did not empower those that could defend her, increasing the amount of passive and assister bystanders. At this broader level, general perceptions and norms affect behaviors (Lindstrom Johnson et al., 2013). As children are likely to copy the behavior of their peers, norms affect aggression levels and school staff responses to bullying, as well as student bystander interventions.

General levels of bullying, regardless of direct involvement as a victim, contribute to fear in other students, which interferes with students' ability to learn (McDougall & Vaillancourt, 2015; Varjas, Henrich, & Meyers, 2009). In classrooms where bullying becomes the norm, students begin to see it as acceptable and do not respond in positive ways as bystanders or seek assistance as victims (Waasdorp, Pas, O'Brennan, & Bradshaw, 2011). On the other hand, when teachers and other school staff proactively respond to bullying (e.g., effectively intervening), youths report feeling safer at school, with fewer instances of bullying, and report that they respond more positively when they encounter bullying (e.g., by seeking adult assistance; Lindstrom Johnson et al., 2013; Waasdorp et al., 2011). For example, in a study that examined over 6,000 high school–age victims of bullying, perceptions that peers or adults in the school were likely to intervene were related to decreased aggressive responses and an increase in seeking help from an adult (Lindstrom Johnson et al., 2013). Specifically, if victims perceive that other students will intervene in bullying, they have a decreased likelihood of responding aggressively to their victimization. Further, if victims perceive that adults will intervene, this increases the likelihood that victims will seek support. Taken together, these findings underscore the importance of those in the periphery (school staff, bystanders) for bullying prevention. Not only can their influence help stop the bullying and provide support, but the norms regarding bullying intervention behaviors can impact how victims respond to the experience and whether victims will seek help from an adult at school (Lindstrom Johnson et al., 2013).

Perceptions of children who bully also shape the behaviors of both students and teachers. In Mai's story, the instigators had clear social power. They were able to manipulate individuals who were not in their immediate social group to turn against her. The ringleader of Mai's bullying was clearly not a marginalized, socially inept student. Two different social roles are often seen for those who use aggressive and bullying behaviors (Farmer & Xie, 2007). They may be socially marginalized (i.e., rejected and/or disliked) or central members of the social network (i.e., popular or socially prominent). The latter use both aggressive and prosocial strategies (such as leadership skills; Waasdorp, Baker, Paskewich, & Leff, 2013) to maintain their social prominence (Mayeux, Sandstrom, & Cillessen, 2008; Waasdorp et al., 2013). Thus, the use of bullying to attain higher social status begins in early elementary school and is especially strong during late childhood and early adolescence (e.g., Cillessen & Borch, 2006; Pellegrini & Long, 2002). Studies of middle and high school youth suggest that the most popular students tend to display the highest levels of overt (e.g., teasing, pushing, threatening, hitting) and relational aggression (e.g., rumor spreading, social exclusion) compared to those with lower social status (e.g., Hoff, Reese-Weber, Schneider, & Stagg, 2009). Relational aggression is particularly important for attaining and maintaining high social status during late childhood and early adolescence (e.g., Cillessen & Mayeux, 2004; Farmer & Xie, 2007). These children use social manipulation to stay at the top of the social tower and often have more social power than popular youths who do not use relational aggression. Therefore, if these popular kids use bullying behaviors to attain and maintain their social influence, they have strong influence on creating a social climate where relational bullying is accepted and readily used (e.g., Reijntjes et al., 2013). In this climate, bystanders are much less likely to intervene and victims are more likely to have social and emotional adjustment difficulties (Garandeau, Wilson, & Rodkin, 2010; Waasdorp et al., 2011).

Even broader school-level factors can impact levels of bullying. For example, a study of 35 elementary schools found that school policies affect individual bullying levels. Specifically, in schools with policies on collecting data and keeping records of bullying (both in and outside school), teachers and parents are more likely to know the policy and students are more likely to report bullying behaviors. Schools with professional development activities focusing on reducing bullying had lower levels of bullying victimization. Further, schools with fully implemented behavior policies (i.e., the program is delivered as intended) that use data collection strategies (e.g., surveys) to ensure that the program is effective had lower levels of bullying victimization. Finally, schools that promote teacher collaboration and positive relationships with parents had lower levels of bullying victimization (Muijs, 2017).

Schools with better disciplinary structures (e.g., rules that are fair and strictly reinforced) and adults who were supportive and caring toward the students had lower levels of teasing and victimization (Cornell, Shukla, & Konold, 2015). Having lower levels of these behaviors improves academic achievement test scores (Lacey & Cornell, 2013). Similar conclusions have been drawn based on other studies (e.g., Konishi, Miyazaki, Hymel, & Waterhouse, 2017; Low & Van Ryzin, 2014), further illustrating the importance of a positive climate for bullying prevention, regardless of the individual-level risk factors (Fink, Patalay, Sharpe, & Wolpert, 2018). Together, these findings suggest that schools need consistent discipline coupled with caring and support for the students by adults, akin to an authoritative model. In such contexts, students' peer-to-peer social climate can improve and bullying will be reduced (Cornell et al., 2015).

The Role of Teachers in Bullying Prevention

Bullying is most likely to occur in school areas where the student-to-teacher ratio is high, such as hallways, lunchrooms, and during recess. However, because children spend a large proportion of their day in the classroom, the vast majority of bullying occurs there (Bradshaw et al., 2007; Demaray, Malecki, Secord, & Lyell, 2013). Thus the classroom is a particularly important context for bullying prevention and intervention, placing teachers on the front line (Demaray et al., 2013). When teachers believe that bullying is a normative experience (e.g., "girls will be girls"), they will likely expect children to resolve bullying conflicts on their own, which can inadvertently worsen bullying behaviors (e.g., Newman, 2003; Troop-Gordon & Ladd, 2015). Teachers' belief that bullying is normative has been directly associated with a lower likelihood of intervening when bullying is witnessed (Kochenderfer-Ladd & Pelletier, 2008), which, in turn, is related to higher levels of bullying in their classrooms (Hektner & Swenson, 2012). This seemed to be the norm in Mai's school, with teachers opting not to directly intervene. Your beliefs about bullying will also influence the type of intervention and advice you give students. For example, believing that bullying is normative or that you are not trained to manage it can lead to passive responses such as telling victims to try to handle it on their own or telling students to leave bullying outside of your classroom; such responses do not reduce levels of aggressive behaviors (Troop-Gordon & Ladd, 2015).

Your relationships with students strongly influence their peer social interactions. For example, when harsh discipline (e.g., physical and verbal punishment, coercion, and intimidation) is used to manage the classroom, it not only influences student perceptions that you are not supportive but can also lead to higher levels of bullying (Banzon-Librojo, Garabiles, & Alampay, 2017). Further, victims of bullying who have poor relationships with their teacher (e.g., low closeness, high conflict) are at an increased risk for psychosocial distress, such as depression, compared to victims who did have good relationships (Huang, Lewis, Cohen, Prewett, & Herman, 2018; Sulkowski & Simmons, 2018). Not only are relationships important for students' social and emotional well-being, especially for victims of bullying, the teacher-student relationship can buffer the academic decline that often results from being a victim of bullying. In a long-term study of third and fourth graders, when there are high levels of peer victimization with positive teacher-student relationships, not only do levels of victimization decline, but poor academic trajectories can be avoided (Troop-Gordon & Kuntz, 2013). Such relationships might be especially important for boys (Konishi, Hymel, Zumbo, & Li, 2010; Waasdorp, Monopoli, Johnson-Horowitz, & Leff, in press). These studies further highlight the crucial role of teachers in mitigating the negative effects of bullying (Espelage, Polanin, & Low, 2014).

Unfortunately, teachers and students differ in their perception of the extent to which teachers intervene effectively. Teachers typically believe they intervene in bullying situations more often than students report (e.g., Newman & Murray, 2005). Plus, students often perceive that teacher intervention makes the situation worse; as a result, students rarely report bullying incidents to school staff and instead tell only their friends (Bradshaw, Waasdorp, et al., 2018; Rigby & Bagshaw, 2003). Given these findings, effective intervention strategies are vital to best help students.

It is important to be aware of any biases that might affect your behaviors. Studies show that school staff are more likely to intervene when they witness physical or direct verbal bullying, and less likely to intervene in relational bullying situations (Begotti, Tirassa, & Acquadro Maran, 2017; Yoon, Sulkowski, & Bauman, 2016). There is a bias or perception that physical or verbal bullying is more serious, which could evoke more empathy for the victims and increase the propensity for adults to intervene only in physical or direct verbal bullying (Begotti et al., 2017; Troop-Gordon & Ladd, 2015). Further, adults have difficulty detecting relational forms of bullying (Leff, Kupersmidt, Patterson, & Power, 1999; Mishna, 2004), especially without the proper training (Bradshaw, Waasdorp, O'Brennan, & Gulemetova, 2013; Bradshaw, Waasdorp, et al., 2018).

As teachers, we might feel that we do not have the skills to effectively handle bullying. For example, we may feel that the school counselor is better equipped to deal with peer difficulties. This belief can translate into not responding (Bradshaw et al., 2013; Bradshaw, Waasdorp, et al., 2018; Veenstra, Lindenberg, Huitsing, Sainio, & Salmivalli, 2014), and we know that failing to respond increases the levels of bullying and overall aggression (Campaert, Nocentini, & Menesini, 2017; Weyns et al., 2017). Further, our own implicit biases, such as our personal beliefs about gender, sexual orientation, or religion, may also lead us to turn a blind eye to certain types of bullying, or respond in ways that inadvertently condone the bullying, such as a teacher telling a gender-nonconforming student, "You wouldn't be bullied if you didn't act that way," or "dress like a girl." Although the teacher may have good intentions, such responses reflect a much deeper implicit bias. We should be aware of such bias to effectively address bullying.

While much of this book has focused on the impact of bullying on students and classrooms, teachers are also impacted by these concerns. Former teachers typically report concerns about classroom management and student discipline problems as top reasons why they chose to leave the field of teaching. Moreover, concerns about their own safety and the negative climate resulting from high rates of bullying make this an issue for teachers' own well-being in schools, not only as agents of intervention but also as actors in the broader school context.

What Can Teachers Do
When Bullying Happens

Deena, a fourth grade teacher, had to step into the hallway to discuss something with another teacher. When she came back into the classroom, the students were out of their seats and chatting with each other. Deena knew that one of her students, Jerome, had been struggling to connect with peers. He looked upset, and Deena caught the tail end of a conversation where one student had teased him for both his clothing and intellect, which resulted in other students laughing. The student then quickly followed the statement with "just playin', Jerome." This was clearly a teachable moment. Deena said "You know, if someone said those things to me, it would hurt, even if you think it was just a joke. In fact, with all these people standing around laughing, it would make me feel even worse." She then reminded the students of the class rules about treating others how you want to be treated, and the power in being an upstander for making the classroom inclusive and accepting.

Given the demands on teachers to help students achieve academically, the salience of peer relationships for their students can often be overlooked. Yet for school-age students, establishing and maintaining peer relationships draws a large proportion of their focus when in school. The expectation that students can leave "drama" (Allen, 2015) related to peer relationships outside of class is often not met (Bradshaw, Waasdorp, et al., 2018). This is especially true when students are having difficulty, such as bullying, within these relationships.

As noted in Chapter 3, teachers are a crucial part of bullying prevention and intervention. While it is clear that they can help reduce bullying, a variety of factors determine whether bullying prevention is prioritized. Teacher training often does not focus on the social and emotional skills of students compared to, for example, the training of school counselors or guidance counselors. While all U.S. schools are mandated to have a policy or procedure related to bullying prevention, teachers are often not trained on these policies (Bradshaw et al., 2013). Further, there are many competing demands for time in school, most of which (if not all) focus on academic skills and knowledge and not on emotional and social skills. Together this might cause us to feel we cannot focus on the social relationships of our students, because we are not trained or there is not enough time. While these barriers are valid, prioritizing SEL has been shown to increase academic engagement (Durlak et al., 2011; Farmer et al., 2017; Garner, 2017). Using an SEL approach to classroom management, the social relationships and emotional interactions in the classroom are a central focus, which in turn helps prevent disruptive social interactions, allowing for more focus on academic instruction.

For example, having strong social and emotional skills is important for kids to successfully navigate bullying (e.g., Smith & Low, 2013). A curriculum that focuses on building the social and emotional skills of students can contribute to more positive social behaviors, increased connection to school, reduced conduct problems and emotional difficulties (Durlak et al., 2011), and can help prevent bullying (Brown, Low, Smith, & Haggerty, 2011; Smith & Low, 2013). While the past decade has seen an increasing focus on promoting students' social and emotional skills, in order to decrease bullying, we need to be sure that teachers are central to this discourse.

Children focus first and foremost on their peer relationships, and difficulties that seem trivial from an adult point of view are catastrophic to children. Teachers must keep in mind that it is extremely difficult for children to "turn off" peer difficulties in the classroom. Creating rules suggesting students "leave the drama outside" the classroom is a common approach. However, interviews with students show that this type of rule is often interpreted as meaning that the teacher doesn't care or doesn't understand (Bradshaw, Waasdorp, et al., 2018). It is therefore crucial for teachers to establish strong relationships with their students while simultaneously creating and enforcing clear rules and expectations regarding social behaviors in the classroom.

What Teachers Can Do to Be More Aware and Connected

It is important to know the roles and forms that bullying can take and to be able to identify bullying behaviors when they occur. A critical first step in this process is becoming more aware of the different forms of bullying and how our own biases might impact the way we view and intervene with bullying behaviors.

Check Your Perceptions

First, ask yourself, "What do I think of as bullying?" If you view bullying as normative, you might feel there is no need to intervene and that children learn how to stand up for themselves or how to successfully handle conflict later in life through bullying experiences (DeOrnellas & Spurgin, 2017; Hektner & Swenson, 2012). However, this type of belief should be challenged. Bullying is not mere conflict. With a strong power differential and repeated behavior, the victim loses power while those who bully gain power. This makes resolving the conflict on their own extremely difficult. With social media as an avenue for bullying behaviors, bullying can feel even more overwhelming and insurmountable for young people.

Next, ask yourself, "What behaviors do I consider to be bullying?" As noted previously, physical bullying is often perceived as the most harmful, needing adult intervention, and more covert forms such as relational bullying are not (Demaray et al., 2013). If you strongly feel that there is no bullying in your classroom, think of social conflicts or disruptive behaviors, especially from your students' point of view. For example, a teacher we interviewed insisted there was no bullying in her classroom; but when pressed to discuss social behaviors or disruptions, told a story about a child in her class that chose to bring small gifts only for certain children, purposefully excluding one particular child. It was clear from the story that this was not an isolated event, and the girl regularly displayed this type of behavior. The teacher did not see this situation as requiring her intervention, other than telling the children to put the gifts away. Unfortunately, this teacher had a bias toward feeling that this type of behavior is normative, leading her to ignore the underlying relational bullying that was occurring. This is especially likely to happen when the relational bullying occurs between girls (e.g., Troop-Gordon & Ladd, 2015). Some may even think that bullying is just a fact of life, and that facing this type of challenge helps them to be stronger—that the bullying "toughens them up". The classroom climate can be impacted if teachers ignore such bullying behaviors, and children may feel that certain behaviors are more socially acceptable, such as rumor spreading, excluding, and other more covert behaviors.

It is also important to reflect on your own involvement in bullying (e.g., as a victim, currently or in childhood), as this can influence perceptions and responses. For example, teachers who were bullies may be more permissive toward bullying behaviors in the classroom, leading to higher levels of bullying (e.g., Oldenburg et al., 2015). Those who were bullies might model negative social behaviors such as teasing or rolling their eyes at certain students, which can increase students' bullying behaviors (DeOrnellas & Spurgin, 2017; Oldenburg et al., 2015). Teachers who were victims might also avoid intervening due to their own negative experiences of being victims. On the other hand, these teachers could be more empathic and motivated to intervene based on their stronger desire to stop this type of behavior. It is therefore important to be cognizant of how your own experiences with bullying could impact your view of children who are involved in bullying.

Identify Behaviors and Respond to All Participants

A second grade teacher, Tre, described a student in his classroom who constantly displayed disruptive behavior and at times bullying behavior. No matter what he did to try to find out the underlying issue, he could not understand what was motivating the student to bully. In the end, Tre discovered that merely being an emotional support was helpful. Tre continued to provide support to this student for years to come. While he felt this emotional support role was outside of his "area of expertise," he wanted to be a person that the student viewed as "there for him." Tre tried to give up an occasional lunch to connect with students who seemed to need additional support. He found this level of connection, improved his overall class climate. His connections with these students have led to other teachers seeing those meetings as important too.

Bullying does not necessarily disrupt the class, which is why it is important to be well versed in the different bullying behaviors, both overt and covert. Even when bullying does disrupt the classroom, it can be difficult to understand the specifics of the situation. As an example, if a teacher is rotating between small groups when a heated argument breaks out, the teacher often misses which roles the students played in the disagreement. In this instance, teachers could first reflect on what they see: "While I did not see what happened, I do see two kids who are both really upset." It is important not to assume you know which role a child played. A child who has had numerous behavioral infractions might be quickly blamed as the instigator of the fight, but it could be that the child was reacting to teasing or exclusion as the victim. Due to the dynamic nature of peer relationships and the systemic nature of bullying, it is important that you briefly connect emotionally with all students involved.

In the moment, there is a tendency to respond to bullying by focusing on the child who is doing the bullying rather than the victim (Burger, Strohmeier, Spröber, Bauman, & Rigby, 2015; Yoon et al., 2016). But it is imperative to show support for the student who is the victim, as this signals to the victim and other students that bullying behavior is not acceptable. Moreover, it conveys to the student who is bullied that the teacher cares about them, and wants to help and improve the situation (Campaert et al., 2017; Garandeau, Vartio, Poskiparta, & Salmivalli, 2016).

Punishing the child who bullied may temporarily stop the bullying, but only in that specific instance. It may not stem the behavior in the long term. It is important to remember in these challenging moments that a child who bullies may also need to connect with an adult who cares and get support to change their behavior. But a punitive response from the adult may further damage their relationship with the student and further drive the student away. This is not to say that bullying behaviors do not warrant reprimands or consequences. But first, model SEL skills by connecting emotionally. Express concern, empathy, and care through validation of the difficult experience the children are having, and then move on to the consequences. In these instances, it is important to indicate you are available and want to discuss the situation outside of class time (in separate meetings with the victim and the perpetrator), saying something such as, "I am so sorry this happened. I will follow up with you and talk about this later today."

In contrast, some teachers might be tempted to use behavioral modification techniques to address bullying. However, some strategies, like planned ignoring (where teachers intentionally ignore negative behaviors in the hope the behaviors will stop on their own) are not likely to be effective and may even be harmful. Moreover, some teachers may be concerned about responding to bullying at all, as that may be perceived by the bullying student as giving them attention, and in turn reinforce the bullying behavior. Although planned ignoring techniques may be effective at stemming other *minor irritating* behavior problems (like disruptions or attention-getting acts like calling out) they should not be used in situations where students are harmed—as is the case in bullying. In fact, when it comes to bullying, ignoring is *not* recommended, as it can be perceived as condoning the bullying behavior. A victim of bullying does not have the physical or social power to stop the bullying, and a teacher ignoring it can be detrimental.

Through an SEL approach you can convey to the class that you care and are available, thwarting students' perceptions that the behavior has been ignored or condoned, yet still do whatever is necessary to stop the bullying from disrupting the classroom.

It is important not to overlook the bystanders in the situation. Do not forget what impact the bullying may have on them, or what influence they may have in resolving or preventing future incidents. Bystanders play an influential role in perpetuating bullying. To most efficiently decrease bullying behaviors, beyond briefly addressing the child who bullied and the victim's needs, focus on the bystander. When you witness bullying in your classroom, take the opportunity to reinforce students' positive bystander or upstander responses, such as sticking up for or comforting the victim, and getting help from adults. Students may also need to be reminded that bystanders should be good friends by not laughing at the bullying, as that can make matters worse and reinforce the bullying. Children often say they were "just playing," making it difficult to distinguish between play and real fighting (e.g., Bradshaw, Waasdorp, et al., 2018; Richards, 2016; Schäfer & Smith, 1996). This is an example of a teachable moment that allows a teacher to briefly model techniques that the children should use when faced with a bullying situation or one that is ambiguous.

Intervene at Teachable Moments

If you see behaviors similar to those Deena witnessed in the vignette at the start of this chapter, where other students are reacting with laughter to the verbal bullying of one of their classmates, it might feel more efficient in the moment to quiet the kids and have them quickly go back to their seats. But looking for teachable moments like these can help prevent behaviors from escalating, will improve the social climate, show the students that you care about their emotions and relationships, and prevent future bullying behaviors. When a child is "just playing," yet name calling, it is important to express that names do hurt, as this fourth grade teacher did.

It is important to note that not all children who bully have a social skill deficit. In fact, social skills may give them the ability to keep the bullying hidden. For example, when relational bullying is used to maintain social status, a student might be adept at being aggressive only when adults aren't around, making detection very difficult. When this is coupled with a bias that relational bullying is not very harmful, these behaviors can go unnoticed far longer than physical or direct verbal bullying. This kind of situation is illustrated in Mai's story at the start of Chapter 3. The instigators did not have social deficits, and used their social power to impact the broader social climate, instilling fear of retribution in others—beyond just Mai. Once bully situations get to this level of intensity, it is even more difficult to intervene. It is therefore important to be aware of comments that allude to more covert relational or cyberbullying in order to prevent these behaviors from escalating.

With the increasing use of social media, children can harm other students psychologically and drastically manipulate their social standing without any adults witnessing this behavior. In a qualitative study of teachers' detection of bullying, when a student pulled out her phone and blatantly showed her neighbor an Instagram post in which someone was being teased for her weight, and the student liked the post and forwarded it, all the teachers in the study responded by telling the child to put the phone away, often citing the rule that phones are not allowed in class. Not one teacher mentioned that the behavior itself was harmful or unacceptable. Essentially, in this example, this bullying behavior was only viewed as a behavioral infraction. It is therefore important to be explicit about what constitutes bullying, labeling the behavior when it is witnessed, and regularly, yet briefly, including discussions about the social climate in the classroom. To summarize, these are the actions teachers can take to be prepared and to respond to bullying when it occurs:

- **Be vigilant, aware, and connected.** Connecting with students is very important when witnessing and responding to bullying, but it is important to establish good relationships early in the school year to foster a socially and emotionally positive environment. Get to know your students and the roles they may play in bullying situations. Recognize that students may shift in and out of different roles in response to a number of contextual and social factors.
- **Consider how your own biases might impact your ability to identify bullying behaviors or your responses.** Know yourself and your own triggers, as your own personal experience with bullying may impact the way you respond in bullying situations. Learn to recognize all the types of bullying behaviors, with the understanding

that kids might use more covert (e.g., non-physical) forms, especially when adults are around; they may also try to get you to dismiss the behavior as a joke or accident.

- **Collect information on the incident.** There is no single profile or characteristic possessed by all children who bully, nor by children who are victims. So it is critical to gather information about bullying incidents, like when it happens, who does it, what form it takes, where it occurs, and who else is involved or contributed to it. This information is more likely to be provided if you know your students and have preexisting authentic relationships with them.
- **Respond to all bullying acts and all participants**. Remember to focus not only on the student who is bullying, but also to address the victim's needs, and finally to include the bystanders—either to reinforce upstander behavior, or if necessary, remind students not to encourage bullying behaviors.
- **Take advantage of "teachable moments."** Take the opportunity when bullying occurs to stop and remind students of the expectations for positive social interactions in the classroom, and to reestablish your caring for all participants; these "teachable moments" will be more effective to prevent bullying than simply resuming other classroom activities without any reference to what has happened.

ACTIVITY TO PROMOTE TEACHERS' SELF-REFLECTIONS RELATED TO BULLYING

(1) Self-Reflection: Explore your own past (or current) experiences with bullying, and understand how your own experience could affect your responses to witnessing student bullying behaviors. Do you perceive that bullying is a normal part of growing up that does not warrant adult intervention?

    Action Step: Challenge the thoughts that could impact your responses to bullying.

(2) Self-Reflection: What are your biases related to children? If certain children get on your nerves, could this change the way you connect, intervene, or respond to them?

    Action Step: Remember that a child is more than his or her actions in a particular moment.

(3) Self-Reflection: If you have a bad day at work, it can be very difficult to leave it at the front door when you walk in your home; this is akin to asking your students to leave their drama outside your classroom. Children and adolescents are less able to compartmentalize their emotions than adults are.

    Action Step: Remember how important peer relationships are to your students and how hard it is to focus academically when they have a social struggle.

What Teachers Can Do to Prevent Bullying

A fifth grade teacher described how she tries to develop a connection and authentic relationship with all of her students so she has a foundation to draw upon when bullying and other problems occur: "I try to get to know my students—I mean really know them. I spend a week during the fall semester focusing on each kid in the class. I fill out a brief inventory of each student's strengths, values, and other personal or family factors. I ask them a series of questions about themselves, like their hobbies, games they like to play, shows they like to watch, and how they spend their weekends. I try to get to know them all personally, both inside and outside of the classroom. This helps me to understand the students on a deeper level, and what might be motivating their behavior. I feel that connecting with my students, in an emotional way, helps them to know they can talk to me about their friendships, and any troubles they might have." She continued to describe how such approaches provide a foundation for talking with students about concerning behaviors, like bullying. "Having an authentic relationship with all my students is a resource I can draw upon when times get tough, and when I am worried about them. It also helps them feel more comfortable coming to me to talk about bullying."

As noted in Chapter 3, positive student-teacher relationships have been linked with more favorable classroom behaviors, which in turn translates into better academic and social outcomes for students. Such relationships are also relevant to bullying prevention. Building positive relationships can improve both behavior and academic outcomes (Bradshaw, Waasdorp, et al., 2018; Pas et al., 2019). Awareness of bullying can help you build a foundation for more communication about bullying and related concerns.

Build Positive Student-Teacher Relationships

It is important to build a common language around SEL, bullying, and peer relationships that you can use to communicate openly with your students about these and other concerns that arise. Using basic strategies like increasing your use of social and emotional language (e.g., label emotions, talk about how to calm down when angry, how to be a good friend and show empathy for others) throughout the year, and specifically in response to bullying, can help also strength relationships. These are critical proactive approaches to preventing bullying before it occurs.

STRATEGIES FOR BUILDING POSITIVE STUDENT-TEACHER RELATIONSHIPS

- Give students an interest inventory or short survey about themselves. Students could interview each other. You can purposefully create new pairs that expand friendship circles (e.g., tell students to select someone they don't usually interact with).

- Help your students create posters about themselves, to highlight similarities and differences.
- Mix up seating for team and group work. Help students who are having difficulty connecting with peers buddy up with more socially skilled students.
- Invite students to talk to you outside of class time, and greet them in the hallway each day.
- Seek student input, by using a suggestion box for feedback, including students in development of rules and consequences.
- Use cultural artifacts that are reflective of the students' backgrounds and signal strong endorsement of and appreciation for diversity.
- Write personalized notes on students' assignments.
- Each week, identify a student you can get to know better, and make notes of their strengths, values, and interests.
- Send written notes home or make positive phone calls to parents to reinforce positive behaviors and their use of SEL skills, like helping others and managing a challenge well.
- Create a class newsletter with positive updates to highlight student success.

Create and Reinforce Classroom Expectations

Bullying can be prevented through setting and consistently reinforcing classroom expectations as well as through modeling and reinforcing positive social and emotional skills. In the beginning of the year, create classroom expectations regarding social interactions. It is a good idea to have the students help to come up with the expectations, which should be posted and referred to often. It is best to limit the list to about three to five rules. Examples of classroom expectations could include using a respectful (or friendly) tone, listening to others, only using positive words about others, valuing the property of others as you do your own, explaining how something makes you feel, helping others when they are hurt, being inclusive, and so on. Think of how it feels to be left out. The classroom expectations should be (1) displayed in the classroom, (2) modeled in your interactions with students and other adults, (3) explicitly taught in the classroom, and (4) positively reinforced if a behavior is displayed and drawn upon as a reminder when the behavior is not displayed. These activities can be connected to school-wide or classroom-wide systems of classroom management, Positive Behavioral Interventions and Supports (PBIS), or other such programming efforts.

STRATEGIES TO MANAGE SOCIAL EXPECTATIONS

- Establish and Post Classroom Guidelines
  - Create a classroom definition of bullying and discuss its differ-

ent forms (relational, verbal, cyberbullying, physical). Use chart paper to create a class poster.

- Set up clear social expectations (with a limit of three to five expectations). For example, be inclusive, be respectful (of ideas and our bodies), and listen to others. It is important to be ready to reiterate these expectations when chances for peer conflict and bullying are higher, such as after lunch/recess.
- Post a visual or acronym like the THINK model. (Is it "Thoughtful, Helpful, Inspiring, Necessary, or Kind?")
- Make sure to consistently include peer relations as a focus in class rules, and provide positive and negative consequences for social behavior you witness in your classroom.
- Teach, Model, Practice, and Reinforce Skills
  - Set aside time for discussions or role-plays around bullying:
    - Have class discussions about bullying and students' specific social challenges.
    - Make a list of appropriate ways to respond to bullying.
    - Use media coverage about bullying to spark conversation and make connections.
  - Teach mini-lessons on specific social skills and model using these skills when you are starting to feel frustrated as well as when you see students get frustrated:
    - Use feelings language and I statements. For example, instead of saying "You better quit calling her dumb, you are acting dumb even talking like that" you could say "I just heard some

mean/hurtful names being used, I can see that she looks sad. It makes me very uncomfortable to hear such horrible things too. Is there something I can help with?"

- Perspective taking and empathy.
- The Golden Rule: "Treat others the way you want to be treated."
- Coping strategies: relaxation, deep breathing, gratitude journals, exercise, calming music.
- Identify SEL elements in existing curriculum and connections between current events that can be discussed in relation to empathy, perspective taking, and effective decision-making. This can occur through the selection of course readings which address or illustrate SEL concepts.
  - Review social expectations at the beginning of each class or when transitioning to social activities.
  - Review characteristics of positive group members. With student input, create a chart with ideas for working well together and the importance of perspective taking.
  - Give behavior-specific praise for the use of SEL skills and efforts to stop bullying or seek help for bullying-related concerns.
- Structure Classroom Routines to Apply Skills
  - Plan lessons that ensure different students work together and the structured application of SEL concepts.
  - Reduce unstructured and unsupervised time, as this creates opportunities for bullying.

- Prepare for smooth transitions by setting clear expectations for positive behavior and using pre-corrections before the transition.

Model Empathy

Strategies to model positive ways to interact with others and to cope with difficult social situations are a crucial piece of an SEL approach to bullying prevention. To model empathy for your students, start by labeling how you feel for the class. Label your emotions (e.g., frustration, anger, sadness) and your students' emotions. When you witness bullying, try to reflect what you see by labeling the students' emotions (e.g., face and body responses): "I see clenched fists and rapid breathing. It looks like you are so angry."

Use "I statements" to model assertive communication skills: "I'm upset to hear what you just said to her. Teasing is never okay. Our class has a rule to use only positive words about others." You can also use such a situation as an opportunity to remind the class of the group's expectations. Adults working with children and adolescents should avoid using sarcasm. Some students may be particularly sensitive to sarcasm, and feel embarrassed by it. For example, if a child says to you, "I promise I will bring my homework in tomorrow," and you reply with sarcasm by saying "Yeah, I have heard that before," this signals your distrust of the student. Also, avoid making jokes or comments about a child's "quirky" behavior or physical appearance. While the intent might be humor, children will likely not view it that way—particularly those who are anxious and high in rejection sensitivity.

Such behaviors are likely interpreted as teasing, setting a precedent that teasing is acceptable in the classroom. Similarly, when stressed, teachers can be short or curt with certain students, may point out a child's error in front of the class, or yell at a student. It is important to keep in mind how powerful and influential your behaviors are; modeling empathy and effective emotional regulation for others should be a priority. These might be critical times to use a "mindful moment" to become more aware of how your own stress and behavior may be negatively perceived by students.

Show Perspective Taking

"My first grade class started to use a 4-color zone of regulation system this year. The chart includes kid-friendly descriptions of emotions and emojis which span from blue, being calm and relaxed, through red, to reflect feeling really hot, stressed, and angry. The colored zones of regulation help me talk with students about emotions, and help them become more self-aware and communicate with others how they are feeling. I could tell the students really got it when they started to tell me I was looking really red one day, and that I might need to take a few minutes in the 'cozy corner,' which is an overstuffed chair in the corner that serves as a safe place for students where they can choose to go when they want to calm down and reflect. I hadn't considered going into the cozy corner as the teacher, but it was really powerful when my first graders used the color zones to tell me I needed a cozy moment get myself in check."

A related SEL competency is perspective taking, which refers to the ability to view a situation from another's point of view. This skill requires empathy and is developed over time. It is usually difficult for early elementary-age children to grasp this concept. However, in developmentally appropriate ways, you can help model perspective taking by discussing how someone else might feel in a situation. This can also be done through introducing literature (e.g., *The Day the Crayons Quit*, by Drew Daywalt; *The True Story of the Three Little Pigs* by Jon Scieszka) which illustrate and apply SEL skills, like perspective taking. A library or Internet search will uncover numerous other developmentally appropriate books to help children learn perspective taking in relation to a number of social situations, like conflict. Try to use social interactions as teachable moments. For example, "You might think you were just playing and not meaning to hurt anyone, but it looks to me like she is sad. How do you think that made her feel?"

It is important that you remember to take the students' perspective too. Recollect how important peer relationships are to students and be careful not to dismiss what might seem tangential to your academic focus. Remember, it is through the increased use of positive social and emotional skills that academic outcomes improve, and therefore, taking the time to focus on these strategies in the beginning of the year is essential. Modeling self-awareness and effective emotion regulation are central SEL components that are especially relevant to bullying. For example, if you feel frustrated, label the emotion and describe to the students how you can tell (perhaps linking with a physical symptom such as tension in your shoulders). Tell the class that you need to take some deep breaths (or count to ten out loud) to calm down before responding or saying something you might regret.

What Teachers Can Do

While preventing bullying behaviors from occurring is the goal, realistically, difficult social interactions will always occur in your classroom, ranging from minor conflict to heated arguments to bullying. The importance of your response to bullying cannot be stressed enough. It not only helps in the moment, but also creates a positive social climate of inclusion and respect. Similar to the model for prevention, responses to bullying also need to include labeling of feelings, empathy, perspective taking, and "I" statements. It is most critical for you to stress to students that you care about their social and emotional well-being and are available if needed. When bullying occurs in the classroom and there is little time for an in-depth response, try taking the following steps:

1. **Reflect** what you are seeing. Be observational, not judgmental, and avoid assumptions. Make sure to be honest: for example, "I didn't see or hear what just happened, but I see two very angry people." "I see one very sad and one very angry person." This is also a good time to mention or reinforce being a positive bystander and using upstander behavior. "It is so hurtful to laugh at comments like that." "It was really great that you comforted her." "I'm glad you tried to stop them from picking on her."

2. **Validate** that it is okay to feel a strong emotion, but not to hurt another. For example, "I understand that you feel frustrated with him, but you cannot hit or call someone names." "I understand that you really want to work with your friends, but in our room it is not okay to make someone feel left out." This is a good time to direct your student to remember classroom expectations.

3. **Connect** with both the perpetrator and the victim. After reflecting and validating, it is important not to go back to teaching immediately. Be sure to reinforce your availability and concern. You can say, "While we do not have time to talk right now, I do care, and I am available to talk with you after class" or "This looks really difficult. I would like to help, so let's find a time to talk." Be sure to distribute attention between both victim and bully, but remember not to meet with them together.

In general, when responding to bullying in the moment, it is important to use affective statements (reflecting feelings, expressing empathy for the victim), help the perpetrator to see another perspective, and especially, show you understand how it feels to be in this difficult situation and want to help. If you feel you lack the skills to help students navigate difficult conflicts, it is important to have resources to give (e.g., help the child connect with the guidance counselor, or find out if your school has an evidence-based program for anger management). A program specifically designed to help teachers detect, intervene, and prevent bullying called the Bullying Classroom Check Up (Bradshaw, O' Brennan, et al.,

2018; Bradshaw, Waasdorp, et al., 2018; Pas et al., 2019) has some additional strategies for teachers.

TIPS FOR RESPONDING TO BULLYING BEHAVIORS

- Create and consistently implement a hierarchy of clear, logical consequences for inappropriate behavior.
- Examine the intent behind the bullying behavior (e.g., to gain popularity or social dominance over others).
- Set up time outside of class to problem solve with students individually.
- Avoid keeping the perpetrator and victim together to avoid hurting the victim further.
- Talk with the student exhibiting the bullying (or teasing, unkind) behavior and ask how they can repair the harm they did. Do not force an apology, but try to inspire reflection.
- Check in with the targets or victims of bullying to see how they are doing and remind them you care and can be trusted.

In summary, it is critical to learn how to detect bullying and be prepared to respond effectively when you witness it, as well as when it is reported to you. While professional development on bullying is common in schools, without ongoing support or coaching, it is unlikely that these efforts will cause behavior change (Domitrovich et al., 2008; Pas, Bradshaw, & Cash, 2014). Explicit training, be it in the form of traditional professional development or individualized coaching, may be critical to increasing detection and effective intervention. Such efforts should be connected and integrated within broader school-wide bullying prevention initiatives and efforts to increase consistent and sustainable implementation of the strategies chosen to address bullying behaviors across multiple school contexts.

What Schools Can Do to Prevent Bullying Before it Happens

Bullying in a classroom is most likely to occur when adult supervision is low and during transitions, such as at the beginning or end of instructional time, and during less structured activities, such as small-group work. This highlights how important effective classroom management is for preventing bullying and other disruptive behaviors. Well-managed classrooms are rated as having a more favorable climate, being safer and more supportive, and having lower rates of aggressive behavior (Bradshaw, 2015; Waasdorp, Bradshaw, & Leaf, 2012), and high equity (Bottiani et al., 2012). In classrooms where teachers set clear expectations, reinforce positive behaviors, engage students in the curriculum, and structure time appropriately throughout the day, negative student behaviors are reduced (Reinke, Herman, & Sprick, 2011). Extending these approaches school-wide through models like Positive Behavioral Interventions and Supports (PBIS), can also help reduce rates of bullying by creating consistent norms of positive behavior and proactive systems that set clear expectations for behavior across grades and classrooms (Waasdorp et al., 2012).

That said, strategies to prevent bullying are typically most effective when used not only in the classroom but also in various locations across the school, like the cafeteria, hallways, and playground, as research suggests that bullying often occurs in these less structured settings. But these programs and strategies should also extend into the bus, the home, and even the community (Bradshaw, 2015; Ttofi & Farrington, 2011). As such, it is critical to include parents, teachers, community members, and other school personnel like bus drivers and cafeteria workers in the prevention efforts. For example, we recently worked with members of the National Education Association—the world's largest teachers' union—to develop materials and tools to help different educators and education support professionals learn to address bullying in their schools. While preventing bullying in a bus or cafeteria may have some unique features, as compared to a classroom, it usually boils down to the same basic principles—which largely focus on the five core social-emotional competencies we have been discussing in this book. Furthermore, increased supervision and monitoring are also critical, as are developing authentic relationships with students and knowing what to do when you see bullying, and not being afraid to respond.

But that can often be easier said than done. So in this chapter, we consider some of the recommended schoolwide practices for preventing and responding to bullying. These practices often take the form of programs that teach children skills for communicating concerns about bullying and managing the stress of bullying, and more proactively engaging with peers to help and support one another. Since this isn't an easy task, students often need multiple activities and opportunities to learn these skills. This more holistic approach to supporting students and helping them develop the skills they need to combat bullying would also help them more broadly to deal with other challenges and stressors they may face.

Support Students Through Tiered Interventions

When you teach a new lesson or a skill—be it math, reading, or a concept like gravity—in a classroom, you know that not all students will get it the first time they hear about it. Some kids do get it right away and are ready almost immediately to apply that skill. Perhaps they even knew that concept before you taught it in class. But other students probably need to hear about it a few times before they learn it, or hear about it, see an example, and do an activity to really learn it. Some kids probably need additional tutoring or a pull-out group to really learn and connect with the concept. The same thing happens with learning social-emotional concepts and skills related to emotion regulation or social skills. Some kids have them already and just need a little bit of scaffolding to apply them in different contexts, like when they are stressed out or upset, or when someone has gotten in their face. But other kids really need more intensive support and practice in using those skills. We call using these different types of skill development a tiered intervention. In reading or special education, this often is referred to as response to intervention, or multitiered interventions and supports. Specific models also include positive behavior supports.

These so-called tiered programs take into consideration the needs of the students, including those with increased risk for involvement in bullying, and those already experiencing the signs and symptoms of bullying (Bradshaw, 2015; Ttofi & Farrington, 2011). This highlights why it is important that all students get access to social-emotional learning, not just those who are considered at risk of being bullied, but also those who might be at risk of bullying others. In this chapter, we consider how multicomponent approaches to bullying can be leveraged to try to prevent bullying before it occurs. We also review some best practices for tiered approaches that you can you use to help stop bullying and begin to address some of the negative impacts. We begin by considering how this multitiered system applies to bullying (Bradshaw, 2015).

This model has three tiers: universal (Tier 1), selective (Tier 2), and indicated (Tier 3). Activities and supports that focus on preventing bullying at the universal level (Tier 1) broadly emphasize the development of social-emotional skills for all students—regardless of their experiences with bullying or their risk profile. Also relevant at this level are broader issues like improving school climate. For example, many schools publicly post policies regarding how to treat others in lots of locations throughout the school—like the classroom, bus, cafeteria, hallways, and playground. A core aspect of this school-wide approach is to help shift the norms about bullying, to help kids support each other rather than feel in competition with each other. We also want to see a norm shift related to increasing positive bystander behaviors—what we refer to as upstanders—the kids who stop and help others out, rather than turning a blind eye to bullying.

Universal or Tier 1 Programs

Universal programs or activities are intended to help out all students, reaching out to all students and school staff to prevent bullying behaviors and increase prosocial behaviors. This approach includes publicly posting school-wide policies, so that kids, teachers, administrators, and even parents know what to do and whom to report bullying to, as well as the consequences of those behaviors. A number of programs have been rigorously tested and shown to be effective at preventing bullying. However, we recommend caution when implementing just a few components of these research-based program, as they may not produce the same effects when implemented in isolation compared to the full package. For example, a single lesson in a 25-lesson set is not likely to produce the same effects as using the entire series. The cost and related resource needs may also serve as barriers to implementing the more rigorously tested evidence-based prevention programs.

Nevertheless, numerous social-emotional programs can be used school-wide to promote positive climate and student interactions. Such programs often include a series of activities or lessons delivered by teachers or school counselors. However, school staff often need training or professional development on how to deliver these lessons. Importantly, they often need coaching or support in delivering them with fidelity or as they were intended. Sometimes those materials need a little tweaking or adapting for different students or classroom settings. For example, if a number of students in your classroom have emotional or behavioral disorders, are on the autism spectrum, or have challenges interacting with peers, those students might need more intensive instruction in these skills. This is often where the Tier 2 selective supports come into play.

Selective or Tier 2 Interventions

More specifically, Tier 2 or selective interventions typically focus on supporting particular children who are at risk for becoming involved with bullying. This might include kids who have difficulty controlling their emotional responses in peer interactions or children who have problems making or keeping friendships, or those who are typically left out on purpose and end up by themselves without many friends around to support them. This tier of programming could include social skills training and emotion regulation approaches delivered in a small-group format for these at-risk children. While the content of these materials may be the same as those used with all students in the classroom, the teaching could differ in the number of times the students review or practice the skills or concepts, or in the level of reinforcement—like specific verbal praise, a ticket, "tootle" (as compared to a "tattle" where a child would report on someone else's bad behavior, a tootle is reinforcing children to report on any positive behaviors they see someone else using), or even a token—they receive this positive recognition for displaying those skills.

Along these lines, teachers may be interested in developing a behavior support program at this tier, whereby the school-wide rules, expectations, or skills are tailored a bit more for these students to work toward. Teachers may check in with these students at the beginning of the day to review the skills, or find it helpful to write them on a behavior support card so the kids can do some of their own progress monitoring. Teachers could also check out with those students at the end of each class or at the end of the day, to review how well they have accomplished those goals. A little summary of their performance on those skills can also be shared with the parents, as another level of reinforcement and to help extend the learning and generalization into the home setting. This type of school-home communication, particularly in relation to their meeting positive goals (rather than reducing discipline problems) is very consistent with a social-emotional approach to supporting students' development.

Indicated or Tier 3 Interventions

The third tier, also called indicated interventions or supports, often includes more intensive programming for kids identified as victims or who bully others. These kids often show early signs of problem behaviors due to their involvement in bullying. Indicated preventive interventions typically address mental and behavioral health concerns and often include the child's family. These interventions are usually more intense and are tailored to meet the needs of these students. They could also include more therapeutic supports for students who have been repeatedly exposed to bullying and other forms of trauma. These types of supports may be beyond the level of expertise or time a classroom teacher has, and thus it's best to get help from a counselor or school psychologist to implement these programs well and without doing further harm. But these more intensive preventive supports are most effective when layered onto Tier 1 and Tier 2 supports. That way all the students are on the same page in terms of their expectations in the classroom. Moreover, these approaches are most successful and sustainable when all school staff are using them in concert with one another, and there is principal support and school-wide buy-in for them. This provides a broader framework for preventing bullying across multiple school settings, and supporting students at varying levels of need.

A MULTITIERED APPROACH TO PREVENT BULLYING

Tier 1: Universal Programming for All Students

- School-wide antibullying policy
- Improving school climate (e.g., safety, student engagement, connectedness among peers, the school environment as a whole)
- Focus on increasing positive bystander and upstander behaviors by shifting norms about bullying
- Professional development for teachers and other school staff on responding to bullying in real time
- Increasing effectiveness of supervision in bullying hot spots (e.g., bus, cafeteria, hallway)
- Informational materials for *all* school staff (including education

support staff, bus drivers, etc.) that describes bullying, including what to do when they see it or their child reports it to them

- Increased monitoring of technology use to limit opportunities for cyberbullying
- Connecting bullying to other school-wide efforts, like PBIS
- Implementing lessons that help teach SEL skills in the classroom

Tier 2: Selective Programming for At-Risk Students

- Pull-out sessions for small groups of students to help support social-emotional skill development and communication
- Bystander programming for more popular or socially influential peers to encourage them to be upstanders rather than passive bystanders
- Small-group SEL training for youths who often rely on aggressive strategies to cope with stress or influence others
- Confidential ways that students can report bullying and related concerns (e.g., online, tip line, drop box)

Tier 3: Indicated Programming Victims or Children Who Bully

- Individual counseling delivered separately for children who bully and those who are bullied
- Family and/or community-based services
- Trauma-informed programming for frequently victimized youth

Data Gathering and Progress Monitoring

We are often asked how we know that a particular approach or program is working. As in many aspects of education, it may be helpful to track progress toward goals. As noted above, individual student progress can be monitored by setting behavioral and skill-focused goals each day and tracking their progress in achieving them—and, importantly, reinforcing them when they meet those goals. Also, tracking disciplinary data, like office discipline referrals or suspensions, can reveal an increasing trend in bullying or related behavior problems. If those data are tracked by location, time of day, form of behavior, and even classroom as well as by student's name, they can be informative for identifying areas that require additional attention and programming.

These types of data may also inform school staff whether a universal or additional tiered program is needed. Whatever program is selected, an important starting point is collecting data to determine need and set reasonable goals toward progress. Another way to do this is to use a survey to gather anonymous student, school staff, and parent data on bullying perceptions and experiences. Researchers often recommend the use of surveys, typically anonymous self-reports, in which they ask students about their experience with bullying. A variety of other methods are currently used to assess bullying, such as observations and peer reports, but such data are typically more burdensome and costly for schools to collect.

Surveys can include questions about location (e.g., Where have you been bullied?) and provide a list of locations around the school. The survey could also ask children to explain what forms of bullying they have witnessed or experienced (e.g., spreading rumors, hitting, kicking, teasing, and name calling). It is important to include items specific to cyberbullying experiences. Although they occur only through electronic devices and not usually during class time, their repercussions can affect behaviors in school. To be sure children understand the difference between conflict and bullying, you can provide a definition of bullying at the top of your survey. You can gather students' reports anonymously by paper, phone, or electronic means (apps, online reporting, etc.).

It is vital that all individuals taking a survey understand the definition of bullying and what behaviors constitute bullying, which can be reviewed through activities such as professional development, classroom lessons, parent workshops, and the sharing of the aggregate survey results. Such data, although anonymous, can be really helpful in identifying potential areas of training for school staff, as well as hot spots or locations where bullying behavior is problematic. These surveys can also capture information on the forms of bullying that children experience, kids' perceptions about how much staff are doing to stop bullying, and even what kids usually do when they are bullied—like get help or fight back. Gathering this type of information is critical for monitoring the impact of bullying prevention programming and the school's progress toward reducing bullying behaviors.

SAMPLE SURVEY QUESTIONS

For Students

- I feel safe going to and from this school. *(strongly disagree to strongly agree)*
- Bullying is a problem at this school. *(strongly disagree to strongly agree)*
- Students at this school try to stop bullying. *(strongly disagree to strongly agree)*
- Adults at this school try to stop bullying. *(strongly disagree to strongly agree)*
- During the past 30 days, how often have you been bullied? *(not at all to 2 or more times in the last month)*
- Where have you been bullied in the past 30 days? *(check all that apply*)*
- In what way were you bullied during the past 30 days? *(check all that apply)*
- What do you usually do if you see another student being bullied *(check all that apply)*

* You can list different locations and leave a blank line for students to fill in locations not listed.

For School Staff

- I feel safe at this school. *(strongly disagree to strongly agree)*

- During the current school year, have you been bullied? *(yes or no)*
- How often have you seen students being bullied within the past 30 days?
- What percentage of students do you think have been bullied two or three times during the past 30 days?
- Where have you seen bullying the past 30 days? *(check all that apply)*
- When you have seen bullying in the past 30 days, how did you respond? *(check all that apply*)*
- Did you feel that your response was effective?
- Have you received training this year on this school's antibullying or bullying prevention policy?

* You can list different responses and leave a blank line to fill in responses not included.

For Parents

- My child feels safe at this school.
- I think that my child's school is doing enough to prevent bullying.
- During the last 30 days, my child has told me that he or she has been bullied.
- In response to my child's most recent bullying situation, I did _____.
- I have received enough information about bullying from this school.
- I would like to receive more information about bullying and what can be done to help increase positive peer interactions.

Support for Teachers to Detect Bullying

Although teachers are in a key position to help curtail bullying behaviors, schools cannot intervene effectively if bullying behaviors go undetected. For a number of reasons noted in earlier chapters, including the covert nature of student bullying and the complex power dynamics in student relationships, teachers often do not detect all the bullying that may be happening in their classrooms or other school locations (Bradshaw et al., 2007). Thus it is important for school leaders to improve detection of bullying throughout the building, and to be sure to treat bullying as a relationship problem, not purely a behavioral problem.

There are activities and behaviors that teachers can utilize to increase the likelihood of detecting bullying, as part of a schoolwide effort. As discussed above, gathering data through the use of a survey can be extremely helpful for detection. Other activities might include peer observation of classroom behaviors, or increasing staff presence in areas of the school or grounds where bullying has been repeatedly witnessed.

STRATEGIES FOR IMPROVING DETECTION
OF BULLYING

- Establish a system for students to communicate concerns and suggestions related to bullying:
  - Create a suggestion box for to report bullying anonymously.

- Remind students they can talk with teachers or administrators privately about what is going on in the classroom or school.
- Consider creating or using a poster that sends a message that reporting to school staff is safe.
- Encourage parents to use the school as a resource. Send a note or letter home listing social expectations and asking parents to help support this by sharing concerns their child reports to them at home.
- Review school climate data to look at staff and student perceptions of bullying.
- Encourage teachers to actively move around the classroom to hear and see better, and to arrange the classroom for maximum visibility.
- Have teachers observe each other's classrooms and record the types of behaviors witnessed.
- Based on survey results about where students say bullying most commonly occurs in the school and what forms it takes, increase staff presence in those settings.

Common Bullying Responses to Avoid

While we all want to do the right thing when confronted with a bullying situation, the right response may not always be clear to us. It is clear that some strategies are more effective than others. Here we review a few strategies that researchers suggest are *not* effective at reducing bullying or stopping it from reoccurring. While some of these may surprise you, others will probably make sense when you consider the reasons why they are not recommended, because they may either increase bullying behaviors or make the situation worse.

1. **Zero-tolerance punitive policies:** These policies and practices are often put in place because schools want to get tough or convey the message that bullying will not be accepted or tolerated. While we understand the motivation behind these policies, the research results are not entirely positive, as these approaches often send mixed messages to kids and families about how these issues will be handled. For example, when a school uses threats of severe punishment (suspensions, expulsions) to address bullying behaviors, such as a three-strike rule or immediate suspension for one offense, this can really deter students, parents, and teachers from trying to get help for the student who bullies. They may not report the behaviors, or may wait until the behaviors are really extreme. But this type of exclusive and punitive response does not address the underlying reasons for bullying, or shift the norm to getting help for skill development—for both the kids who bully and those who are bullied. Rather, it focuses on punishing the child who bullied, when we know that prosocial skills training for the student who bullies is more effective.

2. **Conflict resolution and peer mediation:** While these strategies can help students resolve conflicts, model appropriate social behaviors,

and increase communication skills, this method assumes joint peer-led problem solving. Given that bullying is not merely conflict and includes a power imbalance and repetition, victims often do not have the ability or social power to provide a solution to repeated hostile bullying.

3. **Groups for children who bully:** Having small groups for treating children who display bullying perpetration behaviors (e.g., anger management) has been found to propagate the negative behaviors. Groups that include both prosocial children and children who bully would be more effective. Importantly, children who bully do not always have self-esteem issues, so it is important not to focus on building confidence alone. Some children with strong leadership skills may bully because it brings a desired outcome, like being popular. Other topics include helping children to use their power for good and using their social status and leadership capabilities to improve their relationships with friends and to help out others in need.

4. **Brief assemblies or one-time awareness events:** If a school provides only a quick and simple response such as a school-wide assembly or an awareness-raising hour or pledging event, it is unlikely to decrease bullying behaviors. Similarly, a single teacher may not be able to affect systemic change in the school through these types of events. So a more holistic and systemic approach is needed, whereby the topics of bullying, empathy, and peer relationships should be incorporated into class lessons and highlighted in the curriculum and through daily examples.

5. **Awareness-raising events focused on suicide and bullying:** The media has a tendency to use fear-based approaches, emphasizing a

causal association between suicide and bullying. Schools may take this approach as well to raise awareness of the two complex behaviors. However, there are increasing concerns regarding suicide contagion effects (this is when exposure to suicide or suicidal behaviors within one's peer group or through media reports result in an increase in suicide and suicidal behaviors; Flannery et al., 2016; Holt, Bowman, Alexis, & Murphy, 2018). Schools should be extremely cautious about focusing on this link (see National Academies of Sciences, 2016). Suicide among children is a highly challenging issue with increasing concern. Thus we strongly encourage that you get the advice and help of a mental health expert, guidance counselor, or school psychologist in how best to address this issue with your students.

SUMMARY OF EFFECTIVE STRATEGIES IN SCHOOLS AND CLASSROOMS

1. *Establish clear and consistent policies and rules* concerning bullying behaviors.
2. *Focus on the broader climate*, increase adult supervision, increase adult social and emotional responsivity, and increase positive bystander and upstander behaviors.
3. *Coordinate and integrate bullying prevention efforts* with other programming that is ongoing in a school. It can become a seamless system of support. Schools should have a consistent and

long-term prevention plan that not only includes a focus on bullying but also addresses multiple social, emotional, and behavioral concerns. Instead of having separate programs for each
problem, schools should be sure to carefully integrate programs
and services.

4. *Involve individuals across all systems.* Include all staff at a school
in bullying prevention efforts, including bus drivers, lunchroom
assistants, and nurses, all of whom are often at the front lines
during bullying situations. Be sure to include parents and other
community leaders to create continuity of messages about what
to do in bullying situations—like getting help from adults, not to
bully in return, and to be an upstander, not a bystander to bullying.

Integrating and Sustaining Bullying Prevention Efforts

It is important to consider how schools can integrate bullying prevention efforts with their other existing programs and supports. Research by
Gottfredson and Gottfredson (2001) indicates that, on average, schools are
using about 14 different strategies or programs to prevent violence and promote a safe learning environment. This influx of information and programming can often be overwhelming for school staff to do well, thereby leading
to poor implementation of any particular program and a lot of program turn-
over. Therefore, schools are encouraged to integrate their bullying prevention

efforts with other school-based programming, so that they are coordinated, monitored for high-fidelity implementation, and inclusive of all school staff. Instead of adopting a different program to combat each new problem that emerges, like bullying one year and drugs the next, it is recommended that schools focus on things like SEL that cut across multiple issues for students.

The multitiered approach reviewed in this chapter provides a framework for connecting bullying prevention with other programs to address social-emotional skills within the broader set of behavioral and academic concerns (Walker et al., 1996). Students whose needs are not fully met by a universal bullying prevention program or system of positive behavior support (Sugai & Horner, 2006) would likely need targeted and/or individually tailored preventive interventions based on systematic assessment of their needs (Debnam, Pas, & Bradshaw, 2012; Walker et al., 1996). Through review of data on bullying and school climate, schools can identify core aspects of SEL to focus on and monitor progress toward outcomes. Integration of various bullying prevention and SEL programs may also result in more sustainable changes in the school environment—not only in relation to bullying, but with regard to a range of academic and behavior outcomes that have been linked with social and emotional skills (Durlak et al., 2011). Moreover, by improving school-wide climate and behavior management practices across school settings, these efforts can have a bigger impact on bullying and student outcomes. Furthermore, many of these practices have been shown to reduce the amount of time school staff spend managing discipline problems and increase the amount of instructional time available to teachers (Scott & Barrett, 2004).

Getting buy-in from all students and staff is critical to the success of any bullying prevention effort, especially for school-wide approaches. Not only the fidelity of implementation of the program activities, but also factors like principal leadership, staff attitudes toward the program, and the availability of resources and coaching supports can all impact the outcomes achieved (Domitrovich et al., 2008). Therefore, it is critical that school staff work together in concert to do their homework and preimplementation planning to garner sufficient staff support and buy-in for the program and to integrate the new program with existing supports and services (Limber, 2004).

Once implemented, the collection of fidelity and outcome data is critical to ensuring high-quality implementation, tracking progress toward outcomes, and promoting sustainability. Many schools find it helpful to form a school-wide climate, bullying prevention, or positive behavior support team charged with leading the implementation and helping with program integration and the monitoring process. An implementation specialist or bullying prevention coach can also be helpful in ensuring high-quality implementation of bullying prevention programs. Changing school climate and the culture of bullying is difficult and requires sustained and intensive commitment from all students, staff, families, and the community. It is critical that teachers make a commitment to being part of a larger implementation infrastructure, at the school, district, and state levels, in order to address bullying, school climate, and social and emotional learning.

References

Albdour, M., & Krouse, H. J. (2014). Bullying and victimization among African American Adolescents: A literature review. *Journal of Child and Adolescent Psychiatric Nursing, 27*(2), 68–82. doi:10.1111/jcap.12066

Alhaboby, Z. A., Barnes, J., Evans, H., & Short, E. (2017, July 5). Cyber-victimization of people with chronic conditions and disabilities: A systematic review of scope and impact. *Trauma, Violence, and Abuse.* https://doi.org/10.1177/1524838017717743

Allen, K. P. (2015). "We don't have bullying, but we have drama": Understandings of bullying and related constructs within the social milieu of a U.S. high school. *Journal of Human Behavior in the Social Environment, 25*(3), 159–181. doi:10.1080/10911359.2014.893857

Álvarez-García, D., García, T., & Núñez, J. C. (2015). Predictors of school bullying perpetration in adolescence: A systematic review. *Aggression and Violent Behavior.* http://dx.doi.org/10.1016/j.avb.2015.05.007

Anderson, M., & Jiang, J. (2018, May). Teens, social media and technology 2018. Retrieved from http://assets.pewresearch.org/wp-content/uploads/sites/14/2018/05/31102617/PI_2018.05.31_TeensTech_FINAL.pdf

Arseneault, L. (2018). Annual research review: The persistent and pervasive impact of being bullied in childhood and adolescence: Implications for policy and practice. *Journal of Child Psychology and Psychiatry, 59*(4), 405–421. doi:10.1111/jcpp.12841

Arseneault, L., Milne, B. J., Taylor, A., Adams, F., Delgado, K., Caspi, A., & Moffitt, T. E. (2008). Being bullied as an environmentally mediated contributing factor to children's internalizing problems: A study of twins discordant for victimization. *Archives of Pediatrics and Adolescent Medicine, 162*(2), 145–150. doi:10.1001/archpediatrics.2007.53

Arseneault, L., Walsh, E., Trzesniewski, K., Newcombe, R., Caspi, A., & Moffitt, T. E. (2006). Bullying victimization uniquely contributes to adjustment problems in young children: A nationally representative cohort study. *Pediatrics, 118*, 130–138.

Banzon-Librojo, L. A., Garabiles, M. R., & Alampay, L. P. (2017). Relations between harsh discipline from teachers, perceived teacher support, and bullying victimization among high school students. *Journal of Adolescence, 57*, 18–22. doi:10.1016/j.adolescence.2017.03.001

Begotti, T., Tirassa, M., & Acquadro Maran, D. (2017). School bullying episodes: Attitudes and intervention in pre-service and in-service Italian teachers. *Research Papers in Education, 32*(2), 170–182.

Bistrong, E., Bottiani, J., & Bradshaw, C.P. (2019). Youth reactions to bullying: Exploring the factors associated with students' willingness to intervene. *Journal of School Violence.* https://doi.org/10.1080/15388220.2019.1576048

Bistrong, E., Bradshaw, C., & Morin, H. (2016). Understanding bullying among preschool-aged children. In O. N. Saracho (Ed.), *Contemporary perspectives on research on bullying and victimization in early childhood education* (pp. 61–86). New York: Information Age.

Blake, J. J., Lund, E. M., Zhou, Q., Kwok, O.-M., & Benz, M. R. (2012). National prevalence rates of bully victimization among students with disabilities in the United States. *School Psychology Quarterly, 27*(4), 210–222. doi:10.1037/spq0000008

Blatchford, P., Baines, E., & Pellegrini, A. (2003). The social context of school playground games: Sex and ethnic differences, and changes over time after entry to junior school. *British Journal of Developmental Psychology, 21*(4), 481–505.

Bottiani, J. H., Bradshaw, C. P., Rosenberg, M. S., Hershfeldt, P. A., Pell, K. L., & Debnam, K. J. (2012). Applying double check to response to intervention: Culturally responsive practices for learning disabilities. *Insight on Learning Disabilities: Prevailing Theories to Validated Practices, 9*(1), 93–107.

Boulton, M. J., Smith, P. K., & Cowie, H. (2010). Short-term longitudinal relationships between children's peer victimization/bullying experiences and self-perceptions: Evidence for reciprocity. *School Psychology International, 31*(3), 296–311.

Bradshaw, C. P. (2015). Translating research to practice in bullying prevention. *American Psychologist, 70*(4), 322–332. doi:10.1037/a0039114

Bradshaw, C. P. (Ed.). (2017). *Handbook on bullying prevention: A life course perspective.* Washington, DC: NASW Press.

Bradshaw, C. P., O'Brennan, L. M., Waasdorp, T. E., Pas, E. T., & Leff, S. S. (2018). The new frontier: Leveraging innovative technologies to prevent bullying. In A. Vazsonyi, D. Flannery, & M. DeLisi (Eds.), *Cambridge handbook of violent behavior and aggression* (2nd ed., pp. 724–735). New York: Cambridge University Press.

Bradshaw, C. P., Sawyer, A. L., & O'Brennan, L. M. (2007). Bullying and peer victimization at school: Perceptual differences between students and school staff. *School Psychology Review, 36*(3), 361–382.

Bradshaw, C. P., Waasdorp, T. E., O'Brennan, L., & Gulemetova, M. (2013). Teachers' and education support professionals' perspectives on bullying and prevention: Findings from a National Education Association (NEA) survey. *School Psychology Review, 42*(3), 280–297.

Bradshaw, C. P., Waasdorp, T. E., Pas, E. T., Larson, K. E., & Johnson, S. (2018). Coaching teachers in detection and intervention related to bullying. In J. Gordon (Ed.), *Bullying prevention and intervention at school: Integrating theory and research into best practices* (pp. 53–72). New York: Springer.

Brown, E. C., Low, S., Smith, B. H., & Haggerty, K. P. (2011). Outcomes from a school-randomized controlled trial of Steps to Respect: A bullying prevention program. *School Psychology Review, 40*(3), 423–443.

Burger, C., Strohmeier, D., Spröber, N., Bauman, S., & Rigby, K. (2015). How teachers respond to school bullying: An examination of self-reported intervention strategy use, moderator effects, and concurrent use of multiple strategies. *Teaching and Teacher Education, 51*, 191–202. doi:10.1016/j.tate.2015.07.004

Camodeca, M., & Goossens, F. A. (2005). Aggression, social cognitions, anger and sadness in bullies and victims. *Journal of Child Psychology and Psychiatry, 46*(2), 186–197. doi:10.1111/j.1469-7610.2004.00347.x

Campaert, K., Nocentini, A., & Menesini, E. (2017). The efficacy of teachers' responses to incidents of bullying and victimization: The mediational role of moral disengagement for bullying. *Aggressive Behavior, 43*(5), 483–492. doi:10.1002/ab.21706

Carrera, M. V., DePalma, R., & Lameiras, M. (2011). Toward a more comprehensive understanding of bullying in school settings. *Educational Psychology Review, 23*(4), 479–499.

Cillessen, A. H. N., & Borch, C. (2006). Developmental trajectories of adolescent popularity: A growth curve modelling analysis. *Journal of Adolescence, 29*(6), 935–959. doi:10.1016/j.adolescence.2006.05.005

Cillessen, A. H. N., & Mayeux, L. (2004). From censure to reinforcement: Developmental changes in the association between aggression and social status. *Child Development, 75*(1), 147–163. doi:10.1111/j.1467-8624.2004.00660.x

Cole-Lewis, Y. C., Gipson, P. Y., Opperman, K. J., Arango, A., & King, C. A. (2016). Protective role of religious involvement against depression and suicidal ideation among youth with interpersonal problems. *Journal of Religion and Health, 55*(4), 1172–1188. doi:10.1007/s10943-016-0194-y

Connell, N. M., El Sayed, S., Gonzalez, J. M. R., & Schell-Busey, N. M. (2015). The intersection of perceptions and experiences of bullying by race and ethnicity among middle school students in the United States. *Deviant Behavior, 36*(10), 807–822. doi:10.1080/01639625.2014.977159

Cook, C. R., Williams, K. R., Guerra, N. G., Kim, T. E., & Sadek, S. (2010). Predictors of bullying and victimization in childhood and adolescence: A meta-analytic investigation. *School Psychology Quarterly, 25*(2), 65–83. doi:10.1037/a0020149

Cooley, J. L., & Fite, P. J. (2016). Peer victimization and forms of aggression during middle childhood: The role of emotion regulation. *Journal of Abnormal Child Psychology, 44*(3), 535–546. doi:10.1007/s10802-015-0051-6

Copeland, W. E., Wolke, D., Angold, A., & Costello, E. J. (2013). Adult psychiatric outcomes of bullying and being bullied by peers in childhood and adolescence. *JAMA Psychiatry, 70*(4), 419–426.

Copeland, W. E., Wolke, D., Lereya, S. T., Shanahan, L., Worthman, C., &

Costello, E. J. (2014). Childhood bullying involvement predicts low-grade systemic inflammation into adulthood. *Proceedings of the National Academy of Sciences, 111*(21), 7570–7575.

Core SEL competencies. (n.d.). CASEL. Retrieved from https://casel.org/core -competencies/

Cornell, D., & Bradshaw, C. P. (2015). From a culture of bullying to a climate of support: The evolution of bullying prevention and research. *School Psychology Review, 44*(4), 499–503. doi:10.17105/spr-15-0127.1

Cornell, D., & Limber, S. P. (2015). Law and policy on the concept of bullying at school. *American Psychologist, 70*(4), 333–343. doi:10.1037/a0038558

Cornell, D., Shukla, K., & Konold, T. (2015). Peer victimization and authoritative school climate: A multilevel approach. *Journal of Educational Psychology, 107*(4), 1186–1201. doi:10.1037/edu0000038

Coyne, S. M., Archer, J., & Eslea, M. (2006). "We're not friends anymore! Unless . . .": The frequency and harmfulness of indirect, relational, and social aggression. *Aggressive Behavior, 32*(4), 294–307. doi:10.1002/ab.20126

Coyne, S. M., & Ostrov, J. M. (Eds.). (2018). *The development of relational aggression.* Oxford: Oxford University Press.

Craig, W. M., Pepler, D., & Atlas, R. (2000). Observations of bullying in the playground and in the classroom. *School Psychology International, 21*(1), 22–36.

Craig, W. M., & Pepler, D. J. (1998). Observations of bullying and victimization in the school yard. *Canadian Journal of School Psychology, 13*(2), 41–59.

Crick, N. R., Bigbee, M. A., & Howes, C. (1996). Gender differences in children's normative beliefs about aggression: How do I hurt thee? Let me count the ways. *Child Development, 67*(3), 1003–1014.

Crick, N. R., & Dodge, K. A. (1994). A review and reformulation of social information processing mechanisms in children's social adjustment. *Psychological Bulletin, 115*, 74–101. doi:10.1037/0033-2909.115.1.74

Crick, N. R., & Dodge, K. A. (1996). Social information-processing mechanisms in reactive and proactive aggression. *Child Development, 67*, 993–1002.

Crick, N. R., & Grotpeter, J. K. (1995). Relational aggression, gender, and social-psychological adjustment. *Child Development, 66*(3), 710–722. doi:10.1111/j.1467-8624.1995.tb00900.x

Cross, D., Barnes, A., Papageorgiou, A., Hadwen, K., Hearn, L., & Lester, L. (2015). A social-ecological framework for understanding and reducing cyberbullying behaviours. *Aggression and Violent Behavior, 23*, 109–117. doi:http://dx.doi.org/10.1016/j.avb.2015.05.016

Davis, J. P., Dumas, T. M., Merrin, G. J., Espelage, D. L., Tan, K., Madden, D., & Hong, J. S. (2018). Examining the pathways between bully victimization, depression, academic achievement, and problematic drinking in adolescence. *Psychology of Addictive Behaviors, 32*(6), 605–616. doi:10.1037/adb0000394

Davis, M. H. (1983). Measuring individual differences in empathy: Evidence for a multidimensional approach. *Journal of Personality and Social Psychology, 44*(1), 113–126. doi:http://dx.doi.org/10.1037/0022-3514.44.1.113

Debnam, K. J., Pas, E. T., & Bradshaw, C. P. (2012). Secondary and Tertiary Support Systems in Schools Implementing School-Wide Positive Behavioral Interventions and Supports: A Preliminary Descriptive Analysis. *Journal of Positive Behavior Interventions, 14*(3), 142–152. doi:10.1177/1098300712436844

Demaray, M. K., Malecki, C. K., Secord, S. M., & Lyell, K. M. (2013). Agreement among students', teachers', and parents' perceptions of victimization by bullying. *Children and Youth Services Review, 35*(12), 2091–2100. doi:10.1016/j.childyouth.2013.10.018

DeOrnellas, K., & Spurgin, A. (2017). Teachers' perspectives on bullying. In L. H. Rosen, K. DeOrnellas, & S. R. Scott (Eds.), *Bullying in schools: Perspectives from school staff, students, and parents* (pp. 49–68). New York: Palgrave Macmillan.

Divecha, D., & Brackett, M. (2019). Rethinking school-based bullying prevention through the lens of social and emotional learning: A bioecological perspective. *International Journal of Bullying Prevention.* doi:https://doi.org/10.1007/s42380-019-00019-5

Domitrovich, C. E., Bradshaw, C. P., Poduska, J. M., Hoagwood, K., Buckley, J. A., Olin, S., . . . Ialongo, N. S. (2008). Maximizing the implementation quality of evidence-based preventive interventions in schools: A conceptual framework. *Advances in School Mental Health Promotion, 1*(3), 6–28. doi:10.1080/1754730X.2008.9715730

Donnellan, M. B., Trzesniewski, K. H., Robins, R. W., Moffitt, T. E., & Caspi, A.

(2005). Low self-esteem is related to aggression, antisocial behavior, and delinquency. *Psychological Science, 16*(4), 328–335.

Duong, J., & Bradshaw, C. (2014). Associations between bullying and engaging in aggressive and suicidal behaviors among sexual minority youth: The moderating role of connectedness. *Journal of School Health, 84*(10), 636–645.

Durlak, J. A., Weissberg, R. P., Dymnicki, A. B., Taylor, R. D., & Schellinger, K. B. (2011). The impact of enhancing students' social and emotional learning: A meta-analysis of school-based universal interventions. *Child Development, 82*(1), 405–432. doi:10.1111/j.1467-8624.2010.01564.x

Edalati, H., Afzali, M. H., & Conrod, P. J. (2018). Poor response inhibition and peer victimization: A neurocognitive ecophenotype of risk for adolescent interpersonal aggression. *Journal of Abnormal Psychology, 127*(8): 830–839. doi:10.1037/abn0000380

Eisenberg, N., & Miller, P. A. (1987). The relation of empathy to prosocial and related behaviors. *Psychological Bulletin, 101*(1), 91–119.

Espelage, D. L., De La Rue, L., & Low, S. K. (2015). School-wide bully prevention programs and social-emotional learning approaches to preventing bullying and peer victimization. In P. Goldblum, D. L. Espelage, J. Chu, & B. Bongar (Eds.), *Youth suicide and bullying: Challenges and strategies for prevention and intervention* (pp. 216–230). New York: Oxford University Press.

Espelage, D. L., Hong, J. S., Kim, D. H., & Nan, L. (2018). Empathy, attitude towards bullying, theory-of-mind, and non-physical forms of bully perpetration and victimization among U.S. middle school students. *Child and Youth Care Forum, 47*(1), 45–60. doi:10.1007/s10566-017-9416-z

Espelage, D. L., Polanin, J. R., & Low, S. K. (2014). Teacher and staff perceptions of school environment as predictors of student aggression, victimization, and willingness to intervene in bullying situations. *School Psychology Quarterly, 29*(3), 287–305.

Espelage, D. L., & Swearer, S. M. (2004). *Bullying in American schools: A social-ecological perspective on prevention and intervention.* Mahwah, NJ: Erlbaum.

Espelage, D. L., Van Ryzin, M. J., & Holt, M. K. (2018). Trajectories of bully perpetration across early adolescence: Static risk factors, dynamic covariates, and longitudinal outcomes. *Psychology of Violence, 8*(2), 141–150. doi:10.1037/vio0000095

Estell, D. B., Farmer, T. W., & Cairns, B. D. (2007). Bullies and victims in rural African American youth: Behavioral characteristics and social network placement. *Aggressive Behavior, 33*(2), 145–159. doi:10.1002/20176

Evans, C. B. R., Smokowski, P. R., Rose, R. A., Mercado, M. C., & Marshall, K. J. (2018). Cumulative bullying experiences, adolescent behavioral and mental health, and academic achievement: An integrative model of perpetration, victimization, and bystander behavior. *Journal of Child and Family Studies, 27*. doi:10.1007/s10826-018-1078-4

Faith, M. A., Reed, G., Heppner, C. E., Hamill, L. C., Tarkenton, T. R., & Donewar, C. W. (2015). Bullying in medically fragile youth: A review of risks, protective factors, and recommendations for medical providers. *Journal of Developmental and Behavioral Pediatrics, 36*(4), 285–301.

Farrington, D. P., & Ttofi, M. M. (2011). Bullying as a predictor of offending, violence and later life outcomes. *Criminal Behaviour And Mental Health, 21*(2), 90–98. doi:10.1002/cbm.801

Farmer, T. W., & Xie, H. (2007). Aggression and school social dynamics: The good, the bad, and the ordinary. *Journal of School Psychology, 45*(5), 461–478. doi:10.1016/j.jsp.2007.06.008

Farmer, V. L., Williams, S. M., Mann, J. I., Schofield, G., McPhee, J. C., & Taylor, R. W. (2017). Change of school playground environment on bullying: A randomized controlled trial. *Pediatrics, 139*(5). doi:10.1542/peds.2016-3072

Fink, E., Patalay, P., Sharpe, H., & Wolpert, M. (2018). Child- and school-level predictors of children's bullying behavior: A multilevel analysis in 648 primary schools. *Journal of Educational Psychology, 110*(1), 17–26.

Finkelhor, D., Turner, H. A., Shattuck, A., & Hamby, S. L. (2015). Prevalence of childhood exposure to violence, crime, and abuse: Results from the national survey of children's exposure to violence. *JAMA Pediatrics, 169*(8), 746–754. doi:10.1001/jamapediatrics.2015.0676

Frey, K. S., Hirschstein, M. K., & Guzzo, B. A. (2000). Second step: Preventing aggression by promoting social competence. *Journal of Emotional and Behavioral Disorders, 8*(2), 102–112. doi:10.1177/106342660000800206

Frick, P. J., Ray, J. V., Thornton, L. C., & Kahn, R. E. (2014). Annual research review: A developmental psychopathology approach to understanding callous-unemotional traits in children and adolescents with serious conduct problems. *Journal of Child Psychology and Psychiatry, 55*(6), 532–548. doi:10.1111/jcpp.12152

Garandeau, C. F., Vartio, A., Poskiparta, E., & Salmivalli, C. (2016). School bullies' intention to change behavior following teacher interventions: Effects of empathy arousal, condemning of bullying, and blaming of the perpetrator. *Prevention Science, 17*(8), 1034–1043. doi:10.1007/s11121-016-0712-x

Garandeau, C. F., Wilson, T., & Rodkin, P. C. (2010). The popularity of elementary school bullies in gender and racial context. In S. R. Jimerson, S. M. Swearer, & D. L. Espelage (Eds.), *Handbook of bullying in schools: An international perspective* (pp. 119–136). New York: Routledge/Taylor and Francis.

Garner, P. W. (2017). The role of teachers' social-emotional competence in their beliefs about peer victimization. *Journal of Applied School Psychology, 33*(4), 288–308. doi:10.1080/15377903.2017.1292976

Gibson, J. E., Polad, S., Flaspohler, P. D., & Watts, V. (2016). Social emotional learning and bullying prevention: Why and how integrated implementation may work. In O. N. Saracho (Ed.), *Contemporary perspectives on research on bullying and victimization in early childhood education* (pp. 295–330). Charlotte, NC: Information Age Publishing.

Gibson-Young, L., Martinasek, M. P., Clutter, M., & Forrest, J. (2014). Are students with asthma at increased risk for being a victim of bullying in school or cyberspace? Findings from the 2011 Florida Youth Risk Behavior Survey. *Journal of School Health, 84*(7), 429–434.

Gini, G. (2006). Social cognition and moral cognition in bullying: What's wrong? *Aggressive Behavior, 32*(6), 528–539. doi:10.1002/ab.20153

Gini, G., Pozzoli, T., & Hauser, M. (2011). Bullies have enhanced moral competence to judge relative to victims, but lack moral compassion. *Personality and Individual Differences, 50*(5), 603–608.

Gladden, R. M., Vivolo-Kantor, A. M., Hamburger, M. E., & Lumpkin, C. D. (2014). *Bullying surveillance among youths: Uniform definitions for public health and recommended data elements, version 1.0.* Atlanta: National Center for Injury Prevention and Control, Centers for Disease Control and Prevention, U.S. Department of Education.

Glew, G. M., Fan, M.-Y., Katon, W., Rivara, F. P., & Kernic, M. A. (2005). Bullying, psychosocial adjustment, and academic performance in elementary school. *Archives of Pediatrics and Adolescent Medicine, 159*(11), 1026–1031. doi:10.1001/archpedi.159.11.1026

Goldweber, A., Waasdorp, T. E., & Bradshaw, C. P. (2013). Examining associations between race, urbanicity, and patterns of bullying involvement. *Journal of Youth and Adolescence, 42*(2), 206–219. doi:10.1007/s10964-012-9843-y

Golmaryami, F., Frick, P., Hemphill, S., Kahn, R., Crapanzano, A., Terranova, A., . . . Terranova, A. M. (2016). The social, behavioral, and emotional correlates of bullying and victimization in a school-based sample. *Journal of Abnormal Child Psychology, 44*(2), 381–391. doi:10.1007/s10802-015-9994-x

Goodenow, C., Watson, R. J., Adjei, J., Homma, Y., & Saewyc, E. (2016). Sexual orientation trends and disparities in school bullying and violence-related experiences, 1999–2013. *Psychology of Sexual Orientation and Gender Diversity, 3*(4), 386–396. doi:10.1037/sgd0000188

Gottfredson, G. D., & Gottfredson, D. C. (2001). What schools do to prevent problem behavior and promote safe environments. . *Journal of Educational and Psychological Consultation, 12*, 313–344.

Gray, W. N., Kahhan, N. A., & Janicke, D. M. (2009). Peer victimization and pediatric obesity: A review of the literature. *Psychology in the Schools, 46*(8), 720–727. doi:10.1002/pits.20410

Hall, J. A. (2011). Sex differences in friendship expectations: A meta-analysis. *Journal of Social and Personal Relationships, 28*(6), 723–747. doi:10.1177/0265407510386192

Haltigan, J. D., & Vaillancourt, T. (2014). Joint trajectories of bullying and peer victimization across elementary and middle school and associations with symptoms of psychopathology. *Developmental Psychology, 50*(11), 2426–2436. doi:10.1037/a0038030

Hay, I., & Ashman, A. F. (2003). The development of adolescents' emotional stability and general self-concept: The interplay of parents, peers, and gender. *International Journal of Disability, Development and Education, 50*(1), 77–91.

Hektner, J. M., & Swenson, C. A. (2012). Links from teacher beliefs to peer victimization and bystander intervention: Tests of mediating processes. *Journal of Early Adolescence, 32*(4), 516–536. doi:10.1177/0272431611402502

Hoff, K. E., Reese-Weber, M., Schneider, W. J., & Stagg, J. W. (2009). The association between high status positions and aggressive behavior in early adolescence. *Journal of School Psychology, 47*(6), 395–426. doi:10.1016/j.jsp.2009.07.003

Holt, M. K., Vivolo-Kantor, A. M., Polanin, J. R., Holland, K. M., DeGue, S., Matjasko, J. L., . . . Reid, G. (2015). Bullying and suicidal ideation and behaviors: A meta-analysis. *Pediatrics, 135*(2). doi:10.1542/peds.2014-1864

Hong, J. S., Peguero, A. A., Choi, S., Lanesskog, D., Espelage, D. L., & Lee, N. Y. (2014). Social ecology of bullying and peer victimization of Latino and Asian youth in the United States: A review of the literature. *Journal of School Violence, 13*(3), 315–338. doi:10.1080/15388220.2013.856013

Huang, F. L., & Cornell, D. G. (2016). Question order affects the measurement of bullying victimization among middle school students. *Educational and Psychological Measurement, 76*(5), 724–740. doi:10.1177/0013164415622664

Huang, F. L., Lewis, C., Cohen, D. R., Prewett, S., & Herman, K. (2018). Bullying involvement, teacher-student relationships, and psychosocial outcomes. *School Psychology Quarterly, 33*(2), 223–234. doi:10.1037/spq0000249

Hymel, S., McClure, R., Miller, M., Shumka, E., & Trach, J. (2015). Addressing school bullying: Insights from theories of group processes. *Journal of Applied Developmental Psychology, 37*, 16–24. http://dx.doi.org/10.1016/j.appdev.2014.11.008

Hymel, S., & Swearer, S. M. (2015). Four decades of research on school bullying: An introduction. *American Psychologist, 70*(4), 293–299. doi:10.1037/a0038928

Ialongo, N. S., Vaden-Kiernan, N., & Kellam, S. (1998). Early peer rejection and aggression: Longitudinal relations with adolescent behavior. *Journal of Developmental and Physical Disabilities, 10*(2), 199–213.

Jansen, P. W., Verlinden, M., Berkel, A. D.-v., Mieloo, C. L., Raat, H., Hofman, A., . . . Tiemeier, H. (2014). Teacher and peer reports of overweight and bullying among young primary school children. *Pediatrics, 134*(3), 473–480. doi:10.1542/peds.2013-3274

Jenkins, L. N., Tennant, J. E., & Demaray, M. K. (2018). Executive functioning and bullying participant roles: Differences for boys and girls. *Journal of School Violence, 17*(4), 521–537. doi:10.1080/15388220.2018.1453822

Juvonen, J., & Graham, S. (2014). Bullying in schools: The power of bullies and the plight of victims. *Annual Review of Psychology, 65*(1), 159–185. doi:10.1146/annurev-psych-010213-115030

Kärnä, A., Voeten, M., Poskiparta, E., & Salmivalli, C. (2010). Vulnerable children in varying classroom contexts: Bystanders' behaviors moderate the effects of risk factors on victimization. *Merrill-Palmer Quarterly, 56*(3), 261–282. doi:10.1353/mpq.0.0052

Kochenderfer-Ladd, B., & Pelletier, M. E. (2008). Teachers' views and beliefs about bullying: Influences on classroom management strategies and students' coping with peer victimization. *Journal of School Psychology, 46*(4), 431–453. doi:10.1016/j.jsp.2007.07.005

Konishi, C., Hymel, S., Zumbo, B. D., & Li, Z. (2010). Do school bullying and student-teacher relationships matter for academic achievement? A multilevel analysis. *Canadian Journal of School Psychology, 25*(1), 19–39.

Konishi, C., Miyazaki, Y., Hymel, S., & Waterhouse, T. (2017). Investigating associations between school climate and bullying in secondary schools: Multilevel contextual effects modeling. *School Psychology International, 38*(3), 240–263. doi:10.1177/0143034316688730

Lacey, A., & Cornell, D. (2013). The impact of teasing and bullying on schoolwide academic performance. *Journal of Applied School Psychology, 29*(3), 262–283. doi:10.1080/15377903.2013.806883

Lambe, L. J., Hudson, C. C., Craig, W. M., & Pepler, D. J. (2017). Does defending come with a cost? Examining the psychosocial correlates of defending behaviour among bystanders of bullying in a Canadian sample. *Child Abuse and Neglect, 65*, 112–123. doi:https://doi.org/10.1016/j.chiabu.2017.01.012

Law, D. M., Shapka, J. D., Hymel, S., Olson, B. F., & Waterhouse, T. (2012). The changing face of bullying: An empirical comparison between traditional and internet bullying and victimization. *Computers in Human Behavior, 28*(1), 226–232. doi:http://dx.doi.org/10.1016/j.chb.2011.09.004

Leff, S. S., Kupersmidt, J. B., Patterson, C. J., & Power, T. J. (1999). Factors influencing teacher identification of peer bullies and victims. *School Psychology Review, 28*(3), 505–517.

Levine, E., & Tamburrino, M. (2014). Bullying among young children: Strategies for prevention. *Early Childhood Education Journal, 42*(4), 271–278. doi:10.1007/s10643-013-0600-y

Limber, S. P. (2004). Implementation of the Olweus Bullying Prevention Program in American Schools: Lessons Learned from the Field. In D. L. Espelage & S. M. Swearer (Eds.), *Bullying in American schools: A social-ecological perspective on prevention and intervention* (pp. 351–363). Mahwah, NJ, US: Lawrence Erlbaum Associates Publishers.

Lindstrom Johnson, S., Waasdorp, T. E., Debnam, K., & Bradshaw, C. P. (2013). The role of bystander perceptions and school climate in influencing victims' responses to bullying: To retaliate or seek support? *Journal of Criminology, 2013*(Article ID 780460). doi:10.1155/2013/780460

Litman, L., Costantino, G., Waxman, R., Sanabria-Velez, C., Rodriguez-Guzman, V. M., Lampon-Velez, A., . . . Cruz, T. (2015). Relationship between peer victimization and posttraumatic stress among primary school children. *Journal of Traumatic Stress, 28*(4), 348–354. doi:10.1002/jts.22031

Low, S., & Van Ryzin, M. (2014). The moderating effects of school climate on bullying prevention efforts. *School Psychology Quarterly, 29*(3), 306–319. doi:10.1037/spq0000073

Ma, C. Q., & Huebner, E. S. (2008). Attachment relationships and adolescents' life satisfaction: Some relationships matter more to girls than boys. *Psychology in the Schools, 45*(2), 177–190.

Maccoby, E. E. (1998). *The two sexes: Growing up apart, coming together* (Vol. 5). Cambridge, MA: Harvard University Press.

Martin, C. L., Fabes, R. A., & Hanish, L. D. (2014). Gendered-peer relationships in educational contexts. In L. S. Liben & R. S. Bigler (Eds.), *Advances in child development and behavior: Vol. 47. The role of gender in educational contexts and outcomes* (pp. 151–187). New York: Elsevier.

Martin, C. L., Fabes, R. A., Hanish, L., Leonard, S., & Dinella, L. M. (2011). Experienced and expected similarity to same-gender peers: Moving toward a comprehensive model of gender segregation. *Sex Roles, 65*(5), 421–434. doi:10.1007/s11199-011-0029-y

Martin, C. L., Kornienko, O., Schaefer, D. R., Hanish, L. D., Fabes, R. A., & Goble, P. (2013). The role of sex of peers and gender-typed activities in young children's peer affiliative networks: A longitudinal analysis of selection and influence. *Child Development, 84*(3), 921–937. doi:10.1111/cdev.12032

Mayeux, L., Sandstrom, M. J., & Cillessen, A. H. N. (2008). Is being popular a risky proposition? *Journal of Research on Adolescence, 18*(1), 49–74. doi:10.1111/j.1532-7795.2008.00550.x

Maynard, B. R., Vaughn, M. G., Salas-Wright, C. P., & Vaughn, S. (2016). Bullying victimization among school-aged immigrant youth in the United States. *Journal of Adolescent Health, 58*(3), 337–344. doi:https://doi.org/10.1016/j.jadohealth.2015.11.013

McDougall, P., & Vaillancourt, T. (2015). Long-term adult outcomes of peer victimization in childhood and adolescence: Pathways to adjustment and maladjustment. *American Psychologist, 70*(4), 300–310. doi:10.1037/a0039174

Mehta, C. M., & Strough, J. (2009). Sex segregation in friendships and normative contexts across the life span. *Developmental Review, 29*(3), 201–220.

Mishna, F. (2004). A qualitative study of bullying from multiple perspectives. *Children and Schools, 26*(4), 234–247.

Monks, C. P., & Smith, P. K. (2006). Definitions of bullying: Age differences in understanding of the term, and the role of experience. *British Journal of Developmental Psychology, 24*(4), 801–821.

Moore, S. E., Norman, R. E., Suetani, S., Thomas, H. J., Sly, P. D., & Scott, J. G. (2017). Consequences of bullying victimization in childhood and adolescence: A systematic review and meta-analysis. *World Journal of Psychiatry, 7*(1), 60–76. doi:10.5498/wjp.v7.i1.60

Moffitt, T. E. (2006). Life-course-persistent versus adolescence-limited antisocial behavior. In D. Cicchetti, Cohen, D. J. (Ed.), *Developmental Psychopathology* (Vol. 3, pp. 570–598). Hoboken, NJ: John Wiley & Sons.Muijs, D. (2017). Can schools reduce bullying? The relationship between school characteristics and the prevalence of bullying behaviours. *British Journal of Educational Psychology, 87*(2), 255–272. doi:10.1111/bjep.12148

National Academies of Sciences, E., and Medicine,. (2016). *Preventing Bullying Through Science, Policy, and Practice.* Washington, DC: National Academies Press.

Naudé, H., & Pretorius, E. (2003). Investigating the effects of asthma medication on the cognitive and psychosocial functioning of primary school children with asthma. *Early Child Development and Care, 173*(6), 699–709. doi:10.1080/0300443032000178645

Newman, R. S. (2003). When elementary school students are harassed by peers: A self-regulative perspective on help seeking. *Elementary School Journal, 103*(4), 339–355. doi:10.1086/499730

Newman, R. S., & Murray, B. J. (2005). How students and teachers view the seriousness of peer harassment: When is it appropriate to seek help? *Journal of Educational Psychology, 97*(3), 347–365. doi:10.1037/0022-0663.97.3.347

Noguera, P. A. (2003). The trouble with black boys: The role and influence of environmental and cultural factors on the academic performance of African American males. *Urban Education, 38*(4), 431–459.

Oberle, E., & Schonert-Reichl, K. A. (2017). Social and emotional learning: Recent research and practical strategies for promoting children's social and emotional competence in schools. In J. L. Matson (Ed.), *Handbook of social behavior and skills in children* (pp. 175–197). Cham, Switzerland: Springer International.

O'Brennan, L. M., Bradshaw, C. P., & Sawyer, A. L. (2009). Examining development differences in the social-emotional problems among frequent bullies, victims, and bully/victims. *Psychology in the Schools, 46*(2), 100–115. doi:10.1002/pits.20357

Oldenburg, B., van Duijn, M., Sentse, M., Huitsing, G., van der Ploeg, R., Salmivalli, C., & Veenstra, R. (2015). Teacher characteristics and peer victimization in elementary schools: A classroom-level perspective. *Journal of Abnormal Child Psychology, 43*(1), 33–44.

Olweus, D. (1993). *Bullying at school: What we know and what we can do.* Oxford: Wiley-Blackwell.

Olweus, D. (2012). Cyberbullying: An overrated phenomenon? *European Journal of Developmental Psychology, 9*(5), 520–538. doi:10.1080/17405629.2012.682358

Pas, E., Bradshaw, C., & Cash, A. (2014). Coaching classroom-based preventive interventions. In M. D. Weist, N. A. Lever, C. P. Bradshaw, & J. S. Owens (Eds.), *Handbook of school mental health* (pp. 255–267). New York: Springer US.

Pas, E. T., Waasdorp, T. E., & Bradshaw, C. P. (2018, December). Coaching teachers to detect, prevent, and respond to bullying using mixed-reality simulation: An efficacy study in middle schools. *International Journal of Bullying Prevention*, 1–12. doi:doi.org/10.1007/s42380-018-0003-0

Patchin, J. W., & Hinduja, S. (2012). Cyberbullying: An update and synthesis of the research. In J. W. Patchin & S. Hinduja, *Cyberbullying prevention and response: Expert perspectives* (pp. 13–35). New York: Routledge/Taylor and Francis.

Pellegrini, A. D., & Long, J. D. (2002). A longitudinal study of bullying, dominance, and victimization during the transition from primary school through secondary school. *British Journal of Developmental Psychology, 20*(2), 259–280. doi:10.1348/026151002166442

Pellegrini, A. D., Roseth, C. J., Mliner, S., Bohn, C. M., Van Ryzin, M., Vance, N., . . . Tarullo, A. (2007). Social dominance in preschool classrooms. *Journal of Comparative Psychology, 121*(1), 54–64.

Peskin, M. F., Tortolero, S. R., & Markham, C. M. (2006). Bullying and victimization among black and Hispanic adolescents. *Adolescence, 41*(163), 467–484.

Pinquart, M. (2017). Systematic review: Bullying involvement of children with and without chronic physical illness and/or physical/sensory disability—a meta-analytic comparison with healthy/nondisabled peers. *Journal of Pediatric Psychology, 42*(3), 245–259.

Pöyhönen, V., Juvonen, J., & Salmivalli, C. (2012). Standing up for the victim, siding with the bully or standing by? Bystander responses in bullying situations. *Social Development, 21*(4), 722–741. doi:10.1111/j.1467-9507.2012.00662.x

Puhl, R. M., & Latner, J. D. (2007). Stigma, obesity, and the health of the nation's children. *Psychological Bulletin, 133*(4), 557–580.

Putallaz, M., Grimes, C. L., Foster, K. J., Kupersmidt, J. B., Coie, J. D., & Dearing, K. (2007). Overt and relational aggression and victimization: Multiple perspectives within the school setting. *Journal of School Psychology, 45*(5), 523–547. doi:10.1016/j.jsp.2007.05.003

Reijntjes, A., Kamphuis, J. H., Prinzie, P., & Telch, M. J. (2010). Peer victimization and internalizing problems in children: A meta-analysis of longitudinal studies. *Child Abuse and Neglect, 34*(4), 244–252. doi:10.1016/j.chiabu.2009.07.009

Reijntjes, A., Vermande, M., Olthof, T., Goossens, F. A., Aleva, L., & van der Meulen, M. (2016). Defending victimized peers: Opposing the bully, supporting the victim, or both? *Aggressive Behavior, 42*(6), 585–597. doi:10.1002/ab.21653

Reijntjes, A., Vermande, M., Olthof, T., Goossens, F. A., van de Schoot, R., Aleva, L., & van der Meulen, M. (2013). Costs and benefits of bullying in the context of the peer group: A three wave longitudinal analysis. *Journal of Abnormal Child Psychology, 41*(8), 1217–1229. doi:10.1007/s10802-013-9759-3

Reinke, W. M., Herman, K. C., & Sprick, R. S. (2011). *Motivational interviewing for effective classroom management: The classroom check-up.* New York: Guilford.

Richards, C. (2016). Rough play, play fighting and surveillance: School playgrounds as sites of dissonance, controversy and fun. In C. Richards & A. Burn (Eds.), *Children's games in the new media age* (pp. 99–122). New York: Routledge.

Rigby, K., & Bagshaw, D. (2003). Prospects of adolescent students collaborating with teachers in addressing issues of bullying and conflict in schools. *Educational Psychology, 23*(5), 535–546. doi:10.1080/0144341032000123787

Rivers, I., Poteat, V. P., Noret, N., & Ashurst, N. (2009). Observing bullying at school: The mental health implications of witness status. *School Psychology Quarterly, 24*(4), 211–223. doi:10.1037/a0018164

Rose, A. J., & Asher, S. R. (2017). The social tasks of friendship: Do boys and girls excel in different tasks? *Child Development Perspectives, 11*(1), 3–8. doi:10.1111/cdep.12214

Rose, A. J., & Rudolph, K. D. (2006). A review of sex differences in peer relationship processes: Potential trade-offs for the emotional and behavioral development of girls and boys. *Psychological Bulletin, 132*(1), 98–131. doi:10.1037/0033-2909.132.1.98

Rose, C. A., Slaten, C. D., & Preast, J. L. (2017). Bully perpetration and self-esteem: Examining the relation over time. *Behavioral Disorders, 42*(4), 159–169. doi:10.1177/0198742917715733

Saarento, S., Garandeau, C. F., & Salmivalli, C. (2014). Classroom- and school-level contributions to bullying and victimization: A review. *Journal of Community and Applied Social Psychology, 25*(3), 204–218. doi:10.1002/casp.2207

Sainio, M., Veenstra, R., Huitsing, G., & Salmivalli, C. (2011). Victims and their defenders: A dyadic approach. *International Journal of Behavioral Development, 35*(2), 144–151. doi:10.1177/0165025410378068

Salmivalli, C. (2010). Bullying and the peer group: A review. *Aggression and Violent Behavior, 15*(2), 112–120.

Salmivalli, C., Voeten, M., & Poskiparta, E. (2011). Bystanders matter: Associations between reinforcing, defending, and the frequency of bullying behavior in classrooms. *Journal of Clinical Child and Adolescent Psychology, 40*(5), 668–676. doi:10.1080/15374416.2011.597090

Saracho, O. N. (2017). Bullying prevention strategies in early childhood education. *Early Childhood Education Journal, 45*(4), 453–460. doi:10.1007/s10643-016-0793-y

Sawyer, A. L., Bradshaw, C. P., & O'Brennan, L. M. (2008). Examining ethnic, gender, and developmental differences in the way children report being a victim of "bullying" on self-report measures. *Journal of Adolescent Health, 43*(2), 106–114. doi:10.1016/j.jadohealth.2007.12.011

Schåfer, M., & Smith, P. K. (1996). Teachers' perceptions of play fighting and real fighting in primary school. *Educational Research, 38*(2), 173–181. doi:10.1080 /0013188960380205

Schultze-Krumbholz, A., & Scheithauer, H. (2013). Is cyberbullying related to lack of empathy and social-emotional problems? *International Journal of Developmental Science, 7*(3–4), 161–166.

Schultze-Krumbholz, A., Schultze, M., Zagorscak, P., Wölfer, R., & Scheithauer, H. (2016). Feeling cybervictims' pain—the effect of empathy training on cyberbullying. *Aggressive Behavior, 42*(2), 147–156. doi:10.1002/ab.21613

Scott, T., & Barrett, S. (2004). Using staff and student time engaged in disciplinary procedures to evaluate the impact of school wide PBS. *Journal of positive behavior intervention, 6*(1), 21–27.Seelman, K. L., & Walker, M. B. (2018). Do anti-bullying laws reduce in-school victimization, fear-based absenteeism, and suicidality for lesbian, gay, bisexual, and questioning youth? *Journal of Youth and Adolescence, 47*(11), 2301–2319. doi:10.1007/s10964-018-0904-8

Silberg, J. L., Copeland, W., Linker, J., Moore, A. A., Roberson-Nay, R., & York, T. P. (2016). Psychiatric outcomes of bullying victimization: A study of discordant monozygotic twins. *Psychological Medicine, 46*(9), 1875–1883.

Smith, B. H., & Low, S. (2013). The role of social-emotional learning in bullying prevention efforts. *Theory Into Practice, 52*(4), 280–287. doi:10.1080/00405841 .2013.829731

Solberg, M. E., & Olweus, D. (2003). Prevalence estimation of school bullying with the Olweus Bully/Victim Questionnaire. *Aggressive Behavior, 29*(3), 239–268. doi:10102/ab.10047

Spriggs, A. L., Iannotti, R. J., Nansel, T. R., & Haynie, D. L. (2007). Adolescent bullying involvement and perceived family, peer and school relations: Commonalities and differences across race/ethnicity. *Journal of Adolescent Health, 41*(3), 283–293. doi:10.1016/j.jadohealth.2007.04.009

Sugai, G., & Horner, R. R. (2006). A promising approach for expanding and sustaining School-Wide Positive Behavior Support. *School Psychology Review, 35*(2), 245–259.

Sulkowski, M. L., & Simmons, J. (2018). The protective role of teacher-student relationships against peer victimization and psychosocial distress. *Psychology in the Schools, 55*(2), 137–150. doi:10.1002/pits.22086

Swearer, S. M., Wang, C., Maag, J. W., Siebecker, A. B., & Frerichs, L. J. (2012). Understanding the bullying dynamic among students in special and general education. *Journal of School Psychology, 50*(4), 503–520. doi:10.1016/j.jsp.2012.04.001

Takizawa, R., Maughan, B., & Arseneault, L. (2014). Adult health outcomes of childhood bullying victimization: Evidence from a five-decade longitudinal British birth cohort. *American Journal of Psychiatry, 171*(7), 777–784. doi:10.1176/appi.ajp.2014.13101401

Taylor, R. D., Oberle, E., Durlak, J. A., & Weissberg, R. P. (2017). Promoting positive youth development through school-based social and emotional learning interventions: A meta-analysis of follow-up effects. *Child Development, 88*(4), 1156–1171.

Toomey, R. B., & Russell, S. T. (2016). The role of sexual orientation in school-based victimization: A meta-analysis. *Youth and Society, 48*(2), 176–201. doi:10.1177/0044118x13483778

Troop-Gordon, W. (2017). Peer victimization in adolescence: The nature, progression, and consequences of being bullied within a developmental context. *Journal of Adolescence, 55*, 116–128. doi:https://doi.org/10.1016/j.adolescence.2016.12.012

Troop-Gordon, W., & Kuntz, K. J. (2013). The unique and interactive contributions of peer victimization and teacher-child relationships to children's school adjustment. *Journal of Abnormal Child Psychology, 41*(8), 1191–1202. doi:10.1007/s10802-013-9776-2

Troop-Gordon, W., & Ladd, G. W. (2015). Teachers' victimization-related beliefs and strategies: Associations with students' aggressive behavior and peer victimization. *Journal of Abnormal Child Psychology, 43*(1), 45–60. doi:10.1007/s10802 -013-9840-y

Tsaousis, I. (2016). The relationship of self-esteem to bullying perpetration and peer victimization among schoolchildren and adolescents: A meta-analytic review. *Aggression and Violent Behavior, 31,* 186–199. doi:https://doi.org/10.1016/j.avb .2016.09.005

Ttofi, M. M., Farrington, D. P., & Lösel, F. (2012). School bullying as a predictor of violence later in life: A systematic review and meta-analysis of prospective longitudinal studies. *Aggression and Violent Behavior, 17*(5), 405–418. doi:10.1016 /j.avb.2012.05.002

Ttofi, M. M., & Farrington, D. P. (2011). Effectiveness of school-based programs to reduce bullying: A systematic and meta-analytic review. *Journal of Experimental Criminology, 7*(1), 27-56. doi:10.1007/s11292-010-9109-1

Ttofi, M. M., Farrington, D. P., Lösel, F., & Loeber, R. (2011). Do the victims of school bullies tend to become depressed later in life? A systematic review and meta-analysis of longitudinal studies. *Journal of Aggression, Conflict and Peace Research, 3*(2), 63–73. doi:http://dx.doi.org/10.1108/17596591111132873

Vaillancourt, T., Duku, E., Decatanzaro, D., Macmillan, H., Muir, C., & Schmidt, L. A. (2008). Variation in hypothalamic-pituitary-adrenal axis activity among bullied and non-bullied children. *Aggressive Behavior, 34*(3), 294–305. doi:10.1002/ab.20240

Vaillancourt, T., McDougall, P., Hymel, S., Krygsman, A., Miller, J., Stiver, K., & Davis, C. (2008). Bullying: Are researchers and children/youth talking about the same thing? *International Journal of Behavioral Development, 32*(6), 486–495. doi:10.1177/0165025408095553

Vaillancourt, T., Sanderson, C., Arnold, P., & McDougall, P. (2017). The neurobiology of peer victimization: Longitudinal links to health, genetic risk, and epigenetic mechanisms. In C. P. Bradshaw (Ed.), *Handbook of bullying prevention: A life course perspective* (pp. 35–47). Washington, DC: National Association of Social Workers Press.

Valdebenito, S., Ttofi, M. M., Eisner, M., & Gaffney, H. (2017). Weapon carrying in and out of school among pure bullies, pure victims and bully-victims: A systematic review and meta-analysis of cross-sectional and longitudinal studies.

Aggression and Violent Behavior, 33, 62–77. doi:https://doi.org/10.1016/j.avb.2017
.01.004

van Geel, M., Goemans, A., Zwaanswijk, W., Gini, G., & Vedder, P. (2018). Does peer victimization predict low self-esteem, or does low self-esteem predict peer victimization? Meta-analyses on longitudinal studies. *Developmental Review, 49,* 31–40. doi:https://doi.org/10.1016/j.dr.2018.07.001

van Geel, M., Toprak, F., Goemans, A., Zwaanswijk, W., & Vedder, P. (2017). Are youth psychopathic traits related to bullying? Meta-analyses on callous-unemotional traits, narcissism, and impulsivity. *Child Psychiatry and Human Development, 48*(5), 768–777. doi:10.1007/s10578-016-0701-0

van Geel, M., Vedder, P., & Tanilon, J. (2014). Are overweight and obese youths more often bullied by their peers? A meta-analysis on the relation between weight status and bullying. *International Journal of Obesity, 38*(10), 1263–1267. doi:10.1038/ijo.2014.117

van Noorden, T. H. J., Cillessen, A. H. N., Haselager, G. J. T., Lansu, T. A. M., & Bukowski, W. M. (2017). Bullying involvement and empathy: Child and target characteristics. *Social Development, 26*(2), 248–262. doi:10.1111/sode.12197

van Noorden, T. H. J., Haselager, G. J. T., Cillessen, A. H. N., & Bukowski, W. M. (2015). Empathy and involvement in bullying in children and adolescents: A systematic review. *Journal of Youth and Adolescence, 44*(3), 637–657. doi:10.1007/s10964-014-0135-6

Varjas, K., Henrich, C. C., & Meyers, J. (2009). Urban middle school students' perceptions of bullying, cyberbullying, and school safety. *Journal of School Violence, 8*(2), 159–176.

Veenstra, R., Lindenberg, S., Huitsing, G., Sainio, M., & Salmivalli, C. (2014). The role of teachers in bullying: The relation between antibullying attitudes, efficacy, and efforts to reduce bullying. *Journal of Educational Psychology, 106*(4), 1135–1143. doi:10.1037/a0036110

Verlinden, M., Veenstra, R., Ghassabian, A., Jansen, P. W., Hofman, A., Jaddoe, V. W., . . . Tiemeier, H. (2014). Executive functioning and non-verbal intelligence as predictors of bullying in early elementary school. *Journal of Abnormal Child Psychology, 42*(6), 953–966. doi:10.1007/s10802-013-9832-y

Waasdorp, T. E., Baker, C. N., Paskewich, B. S., & Leff, S. S. (2013). The association between forms of aggression, leadership, and social status among urban youth. *Journal of Youth and Adolescence, 42*(2), 263–274. doi:10.1007/s10964-012-9837-9

Waasdorp, T. E., & Bradshaw, C. P. (2015). The overlap between cyberbullying and traditional bullying. *Journal of Adolescent Health, 56*, 483–488. doi:http://dx.doi.org/10.1016/j.jadohealth.2014.12.002

Waasdorp, T. E., & Bradshaw, C. P. (2018). Examining variation in adolescent bystanders' responses to bullying. *School Psychology Review, 47*(1), 18–33. doi:10.17105/SPR-2017-0081.V47-1

Waasdorp, T. E., Bradshaw, C. P., & Leaf, P. J. (2012). The impact of schoolwide positive behavioral interventions and supports on bullying and peer rejection: A randomized controlled effectiveness trial. *Archives of Pediatrics and Adolescent Medicine, 166*(2), 149–156. doi:10.1001/archpediatrics.2011.755

Waasdorp, T. E., Horowitz-Johnson, Z., & Leff, S. S. (2017). Cyberbullying across the lifespan: Risk factors and consequences. In C. P. Bradshaw (Ed.), *Handbook of bullying prevention: A lifecourse perspective.* Washington, DC: National Association of Social Workers Press.

Waasdorp, T. E., Mehari, K. R., & Bradshaw, C. P. (2017). Research on family experiences with cyberbullying. In S. W. Browning & B. Van Eeden-Moorefield (Eds.), *Contemporary families at the nexus of research and practice* (pp. 240–255). New York: Taylor and Francis.

Waasdorp, T. E., Mehari, K. R., & Bradshaw, C. P. (2018). Obese and overweight youth: Risk for experiencing bullying victimization and internalizing symptoms. *American Journal of Orthopsychiatry, 88*(4), 483–491. doi:http://dx.doi.org/10.1037/ort0000294

Waasdorp, T. E., Mehari, K. R., Milam, A. J., & Bradshaw, C. P. (2018). Health-related risks for involvement in bullying among middle and high schoolers. *Journal of Child and Family Studies.* doi:https://doi.org/10.1007/s10826-018-1260-8

Waasdorp, T. E., Monopoli, J., Johnson-Horowitz, Z., & Leff, S. S. (in press). Peer sympathy for bullied youth: Individual and classroom considerations. *School Psychology Review.*

Waasdorp, T. E., Pas, E. T., O' Brennan, L. M., & Bradshaw, C. P. (2011). A multilevel perspective on the climate of bullying: Discrepancies among students, school staff, and parents. *Journal of School Violence, 10*(2), 115–132. doi:10.1080/15388 220.2010.539164

Waasdorp, T. E., Pas, E. T., Zablotsky, B., & Bradshaw, C. P. (2017). Ten-year trends in bullying and related attitudes among 4th- to 12th graders. *Pediatrics, 139*(6), 1–8. doi:10.1542/peds.2016-2615

Wachs, S., & Wright, M. F. (2018, June 27). Bullying and alexithymia: Are there differences between traditional, cyber, combined bullies, and nonbullies in reading their own emotions? *Criminal Behaviour and Mental Health.* doi:10.1002 /cbm.2083

Walker, H. M., Horner, R. H., Sugai, G., Bullis, M., Sprague, J. R., Bricker, D., & Kaufman, M. J. (1996). Integrated approaches to preventing antisocial behavior patterns among school-age children and youth. *Journal of Emotional and Behavioral Disorders, 4*, 194–209.

Wang, J., Iannotti, R. J., & Nansel, T. R. (2009). School bullying among adolescents in the United States: Physical, verbal, relational, and cyber. *Journal of Adolescent Health, 45*(4), 368–375. doi:10.1016/j.jadohealth.2009.03.021

Weyns, T., Verschueren, K., Leflot, G., Onghena, P., Wouters, S., & Colpin, H. (2017). The role of teacher behavior in children's relational aggression development: A five-wave longitudinal study. *Journal of School Psychology, 64*(Suppl. C), 17–27. doi:https://doi.org/10.1016/j.jsp.2017.04.008

Wildhaber, J., Carroll, W. D., & Brand, P. L. (2012). Global impact of asthma on children and adolescents' daily lives: The room to breathe survey. *Pediatric Pulmonology, 47*(4), 346–357.

Williford, A., Elledge, L. C., Boulton, A. J., DePaolis, K. J., Little, T. D., & Salmivalli, C. (2013). Effects of the KiVa Antibullying Program on cyberbullying and cybervictimization frequency among Finnish youth. *Journal of Clinical Child and Adolescent Psychology, 42*(6), 820–833. doi:10.1080/15374416.2013.787623

Wolke, D., Copeland, W. E., Angold, A., & Costello, E. J. (2013). Impact of bullying in childhood on adult health, wealth, crime, and social outcomes. *Psychological Science, 24*(10), 1958–1970. doi:10.1177/0956797613481608

Ybarra, M. L., Mitchell, K. J., Kosciw, J. G., & Korchmaros, J. D. (2015). Understanding linkages between bullying and suicidal ideation in a national sample of LGB and heterosexual youth in the United States. *Prevention Science, 16*(3), 451–462. doi:10.1007/s11121-014-0510-2

Yoder, N. (2014). Teaching the whole child: Instructional practices that support social and emotional learning in three teacher evaluation frameworks. Washington, DC: American Institutes for Research Center on Great Teachers and Leaders.

Yoon, J., Sulkowski, M. L., & Bauman, S. A. (2016). Teachers' responses to bullying incidents: Effects of teacher characteristics and contexts. *Journal of School Violence, 15*(1), 91–113. doi:10.1080/15388220.2014.963592

Zhang, J., Musu-Gillette, L., & Oudekerk, B. (2016). *Indicators of school crime and safety: 2015.* NCES 2016-079/NCJ 249758. Washington, DC: National Center for Education Statistics, U.S. Department of Education, and Bureau of Justice Statistics. Retrieved from http://nces.ed.gov

Zins, J. E., Bloodworth, M. R., Weissberg, R. P., & Walberg, H. J. (2004). The scientific base linking social and emotional learning to school success. In J. E. Zins, R. P. Weissberg, M. C. Wang, & H. J. Walberg (Eds.), *Building academic success on social and emotional learning: What does the research say?* (pp. 3–22). New York: Teachers College.

Zins, J. E., Payton, J. W., Weissberg, R. P., & O'Brien, M. U. (2007). Social and emotional learning for successful school performance. In G. Matthews, M. Zeidner, & R. D. Roberts (Eds.), *The science of emotional intelligence: Knowns and unknowns* (pp. 376–395). New York: Oxford University Press.

Zych, I., Baldry, A. C., Farrington, D. P., & Llorent, V. J. (2018). Are children involved in cyberbullying low on empathy? A systematic review and meta-analysis of research on empathy versus different cyberbullying roles. *Aggression and Violent Behavior.* doi:10.1016/j.avb.2018.03.004

Index

About the Authors

Catherine P. Bradshaw, Ph.D., M.Ed., is a Professor and the Senior Associate Dean for Research and Faculty Development at the Curry School of Education and Human Development at the University of Virginia. She also codirects two research centers at the Johns Hopkins School of Public Health. She collaborates on research examining bullying and school climate; development of aggressive and problem behaviors; emotional and behavioral disorders; and the design, evaluation, and implementation of evidence-based prevention programs in schools. She has published over 250 articles and chapters and has received several federal grants and awards for research on school-based prevention programming.

Tracy Evian Waasdorp, Ph.D., M.Ed., is a Research Scientist at the Children's Hospital of Philadelphia's Center for the Study and Prevention of Violence. Dr. Waasdorp's research focuses on forms of school-based bullying, aggression, and peer victimization (e.g., relational aggression, cyberbullying, and bystander behaviors). She examines teacher and parent perceptions and responses to bullying, as well as school safety, climate, and connectedness. She codevelops and validates a variety of school-based programming focusing on preventing aggression in youth, and helping teachers to detect, prevent, and respond to bullying. Dr. Waasdorp collaborates on numerous federal, foundation and other grant awards to improve school-aged children's social and emotional health.